WITHDRAWN

S0-ANF-386

WITHDRAWN

FOR USE IN THE LIBRARY ONLY

Ref
ZZ
264.3
.H36
1990

NUCLEAR WEAPONS

in the
University
Classroom

An Interdisciplinary Teaching Reference

Michael S. Hamilton
University of Southern Maine • Portland, Maine
William A. Lindeke
University of Lowell • Lowell, Massachusetts
John MacDougall
University of Lowell • Lowell, Massachusetts

UNIVERSITY
PRESS OF
AMERICA

511760

Lanham • New York • London

Copyright © 1990 by
University Press of America®, Inc.
4720 Boston Way
Lanham, Maryland 20706

3 Henrietta Street
London WC2E 8LU England

All rights reserved
Printed in the United States of America
British Cataloging in Publication Information Available

Library of Congress Cataloging-in-Publication Data

Hamilton, Michael S.
Nuclear weapons in the university classroom : an
interdisciplinary teaching reference / Michael S. Hamilton,
William A. Lindeke, John MacDougall.
p.   cm.
Includes bibliographical references.
1. Nuclear weapons—Study and teaching (Higher).   2. Nuclear
weapons—Study and teaching (Higher)—United States.
3. Nuclear warfare—Study and teaching (Higher).   4. Nuclear
warfare—Study and teaching (Higher)—United States.
I. Lindeke, William A.   II. MacDougall, John.   III. Title.
U264.3.H36   1990   327.1'74—dc20   89–77083 CIP

ISBN 0–8191–7742–3 (alk. paper)

The paper used in this publication meets the minimum requirements of
American National Standard for Information Sciences—Permanence
of Paper for Printed Library Materials, ANSI Z39.48–1984.

ACKNOWLEDGMENTS

Many friends, students and colleagues contributed directly and indirectly to our thinking about this book, for which they deserve and receive our deepest appreciation. Financial assistance was provided by the College of Arts and Sciences, University of Southern Maine during preparation of Chapters 1 and 4, for which appreciation is due former Dean Stephen J. Reno. Grace Hague, an undergraduate political science student at the University of Southern Maine provided research assistance for Chapter 4. Responsibility for the content of this book rests solely with the authors.

TABLE OF CONTENTS

LIST OF TABLES

INTRODUCTION

Teaching about the social and political implications of development and stockpiling of nuclear weapons is, at best, difficult. Nuclear arms education is a complex subject, often raising issues of moral and political choice which require the translation of technical information into terms comprehensible to a general audience. Organizing relevant information and insights from the scholarship of political science, physics, nuclear engineering, history, philosophy, chemistry, economics, law, sociology, art, literature, music, mathematics, psychology, medicine, and atmospheric science is a task far beyond the disciplinary expertise of most individuals.

Courses concerning a variety of social issues raised by the use of nuclear weapons are now commonplace in institutions of higher education in the United States. Such courses may be found in several different departments, from graduate programs in large public and private universities to undergraduate offerings in small liberal arts and community colleges. Some utilize the approaches and insights of a single discipline such as political science or physics, while many others draw on the perspectives of two or more disciplines in attempts to provide an interdisciplinary approach to the subject matter.

Opportunities for faculty teaching such courses to "compare notes" with their peers at other institutions are not common, but do occur. For several years the Defense and Arms Control Studies Program at the Center for International Studies, Massachusetts Institute of Technology, and the Center for Science and International Affairs, John F. Kennedy School of Government, Harvard University have jointly presented a Summer Program on Nuclear Weapons and Arms Control for faculty teaching courses about nuclear weapons. Similar programs have been conducted at the Institute on Global Conflict and Cooperation of the University of California, San Diego. This book owes much to the Harvard/M.I.T. program, in which Michael Hamilton and William Lindeke participated during summer, 1986.

Nuclear Weapons in the University Classroom

It was evident during this experience that
faculty with diverse expertise and resources had
developed many innovative and valuable approaches to
teaching about nuclear weapons. Teaching materials and
methods discussed by participants revealed a diversity
of perspectives not evident in any single publication
on nuclear education. Subsequent research revealed a
lack of any published attempt to systematically survey
this diversity, or to make associated teaching
materials available to the broad audience of faculty
offering such courses. This book is intended to fill
the need for a teaching reference for persons offering
courses on nuclear weapons.

With the intention of sharing this research and
the benefits of the Harvard/M.I.T. Summer Program more
broadly among interested faculty in the region, conference papers were prepared by Michael Hamilton on
"Teaching Nuclear Issues: An Analysis of 52 University
Syllabi" and by William Lindeke on "Nuclear Weapons,
Arms Control and Current Pedagogy." These papers were
presented at the 1987 annual meeting of the New England
Political Science Association, Cambridge, Massachusetts, at a panel on "National Security, Nuclear Weapons and Current Pedagogy" chaired by Professor Lindeke,
and provided early drafts of material which appears below in Chapters 1 and 2, respectively. A preliminary
but partial report of research conducted for Chapter 1
appeared at: Michael S. Hamilton, "Multidisciplinary
Teaching About Nuclear Arms," Journal of College Science Teaching 58 (March/April 1989): 318-23.

The book is also informed by our own teaching
about nuclear and defense issues and the importance
that we place on that activity. It is our hope that
this book will stimulate others to consider diverse approaches to teaching and thinking about nuclear weapons. In so doing we wish to contribute to the improve-
ment of teaching about this subject.

Courses and literature about nuclear weapons will
continue to expand in American and foreign universities. That the field is a major growth industry is indicated by the continued stream of books, films and
journals that cover the subject. As more students and
teachers are drawn to it, more attention must be given
to pedagogy, as well as content. In what follows we
have attempted to raise questions about current
pedagogy in such courses, and have suggested alterna-

tives for consideration that will be worthy of the serious subject they address. We have also provided a
selected bibliography of readings which will be useful
in bolstering the content of such courses.

In the first chapter, Michael Hamilton provides a
context for the other contributions. The literature on
teaching about nuclear issues is briefly reviewed and
judged sparse, with no systematic analysis of how the
insights and special knowledge of several academic disciplines have been organized and communicated to students in colleges and universities. An analysis of
topics and teaching methods used in 75 university
courses dealing with nuclear arms is presented. The
frequency with which technological, strategic and historical factors concerning the nuclear arms race received treatment in these courses is assessed. Moral
responsibility and political choice are found to receive more emphasis than expected, with more treatment
than historical factors. Professor Hamilton concludes
that discussions of moral responsibility are associated
with a multidisciplinary teaching approach, team teaching and use of guest speakers in the courses examined.
Further, he questions whether the number of lecturers
in some courses has not become excessive, sacrificing
coherence in presentation of course content to obtain
multidisciplinary expertise in instructors.

In Chapter 2, William Lindeke emphasizes the disciplinary contributions of political science to nuclear
education. Contrary to the commonplace assumption that
nuclear weapons issues are military or technical in nature, amenable only to expert analyses, Professor
Lindeke asserts that complicated and often arcane discussions of national security and arms control are
really about very ordinary political issues. Resulting
policies are determined by political factors more than
by their strictly technical or military dimensions.
These political factors are identified and presented as
a focus for teaching undergraduate courses concerning
nuclear weapons, and for introducing these issues into
other courses in political science.

John MacDougall approaches teaching about nuclear
weapons from a sociological perspective in Chapter 3.
Professor MacDougall describes his efforts to increase
students' awareness of value choices and cultural factors underlying national policies concerning development and stockpiling of nuclear weapons. The utility

of classroom activities such as small group discussions and role-playing during decision making simulations is discussed.

In Chapter 4, Michael Hamilton presents a selected bibliography of required readings and films, compiled from 75 syllabi for courses concerning nuclear arms taught at universities throughout the United States. A brief introduction highlights readings most frequently assigned in the syllabi examined. The bibliography includes over 800 references, grouped by subject headings corresponding to course topics in syllabi discussed in Chapter 1.

The importance of nuclear education is evident in the variety of discipline-based and interdisciplinary courses currently being offered in university and college curriculums. Likewise, the growing number of advanced degree programs, undergraduate degree and minor programs that touch on these subjects indicate broad concern. Therefore, this book will be of particular interest to political scientists and faculty in history, economics, public finance, sociology, the humanities, national security, physics, and engineering who teach interdisciplinary courses about nuclear weapons.

Michael S. Hamilton

William A. Lindeke

September, 1989

CHAPTER 1: TEACHING ABOUT NUCLEAR ARMS: A SURVEY

Michael S. Hamilton

University of Southern Maine

How can college and university faculty acquire and communicate the special knowledge of several academic disciplines needed by students to comprehend complex social issues raised by our use of nuclear technology? Recognizing that perspectives and insights of the social sciences, arts, humanities and natural sciences may all be useful in analyzing these issues, how can they be organized with sufficient expertise and sensitivity to provide students with a credible learning experience? These questions have troubled faculty developing courses concerning nuclear weapons and society, often requiring laborious efforts at self-education and search for appropriate course materials.

Curricular materials concerning nuclear arms and society are now plentiful, if somewhat uneven in quality. Experience in teaching about nuclear issues is accumulating. Preliminary assessments of the extent to which public school social studies teachers address nuclear issues have been reported (Hahn 1985). Yet little has been published which reveals systematic analysis of how the insights and special knowledge of several disciplines have been organized and communicated to students in colleges and universities (Hamilton 1989). This chapter reports results of such an exploratory study of 75 university syllabi for courses dealing with nuclear arms. This analysis should be particularly useful to teachers developing new courses or contemplating revision of an existing course.

LITERATURE

In recent years, a small number of articles on teaching about nuclear arms have appeared in college teaching periodicals, most often describing a single course, (Schroeer 1983; Saperstein 1983; Ringler 1983; Durch 1983; Ehrlich 1983; Harrison 1985; Winder and Stanitis 1988). Symposia of such articles have been published by Journal of College Science Teaching

1

(1983), <u>Physics Today</u> (1983), <u>Harvard Educational Review</u> (1984) and <u>Teaching Political Science</u> (1987). These include essays advocating a particular approach or inclusion of specific topics in such courses.

Useful collections of university syllabi have been published, but without much attempt to organize them analytically (Alexander 1984; Wein 1984; Federation of American Scientists 1984; United Campuses to Prevent Nuclear War 1984; Ehrlich 1987). The <u>Bulletin of the Atomic Scientists</u> (1984) published an especially useful teaching guide containing short articles on a broad range of disciplinary contributions to study of nuclear issues, and excellent resources for course materials and guest speakers. Yet a recent study of institutional responses to the threat of nuclear war concluded the role of the university remains inadequate and substantial additional efforts are warranted (Kohn and Badash 1988).

The literature is thus somewhat long on cases, but short on analysis of multiple cases. Missing from this literature is any attempt to survey and review several courses on nuclear arms to identify common elements or difficulties in delivering a coherent course while drawing on the knowledge and critical insights of two or more academic disciplines. The study reported here constitutes a first attempt to address this gap in the literature on nuclear education.

DATA BASE

For this study, over 100 syllabi were obtained through a literature search and personal correspondence, with cooperation of managers of the Harvard/M.I.T. Summer Program on Nuclear Weapons and Arms Control, and the University of California Institute on Global Conflict and Cooperation. Seventy-five syllabi for courses taught since 1982 (65 undergraduate, 10 graduate) from fifty-nine colleges and universities scattered across the United States provided sufficient information to warrant inclusion in this study.

These syllabi describe a broad range of approaches, including specially designed courses which survey several disciplinary perspectives on nuclear technology, and more conventional discipline-based courses in international politics or national security policy. The data set represents courses of several active scholars, and some of the more widely-known educational institutions in the nation. (1)

The purpose of this study was to identify topics covered, approaches and teaching materials actually used by some of the most knowledgeable faculty teaching on this subject, and to organize this information to make it accessible and useful to others with similar teaching interests. While some caution is therefore warranted in generalizing these results to a larger universe, their great suggestive value is instructive to persons developing or revising similar courses.

Syllabi were examined to determine whether each course was taught by an individual or a team, the extent guest speakers and films were utilized, whether a course was discipline-based or multidisciplinary in nature, and what topics were addressed. Nominal-level variables were coded for statistical analysis of these characteristics. Joint frequency distributions were examined for these variables using both chi-square based and proportional reduction in error measures of association.

Organizational "Home"

Courses which were listed for credit in more than one academic department were placed with those which had no disciplinary home in the "interdisciplinary" category in Table 1.

TABLE 1

Organizational "Home" for Courses Examined

	N	%
"Interdisciplinary"	29	(39)
Social Sciences	28	(37)
Natural Sciences	7	(9)
Humanities and Arts	7	(9)
Military Studies	4	(5)
	75	(100)

Although most courses in this category were described in their respective syllabi as interdisciplinary, it was not possible in this study to ascertain whether the implied goal of an interdisciplinary synthesis of course content was actually achieved. Information included in course syllabi did not provide an adequate basis upon which to form conclusions on this issue. The term "interdisciplinary" is therefore used in Table 1 as a convenient organizational label which may not be an accurate description of course content actually delivered.

The social sciences provided an organizational "home" for the second greatest number of courses in Table 1. Political science departments housed 20 (27%), the largest portion of discipline-based courses examined.

Multidisciplinary Approach

Syllabi were examined to ascertain whether courses were taught utilizing a disciplinary or multidisciplinary approach to the subject matter. Courses which were described in the syllabi as interdisciplinary (including some having a disciplinary "home" above and offered by individuals), or which were taught by persons from more than one academic department were categorized as multidisciplinary. Under this decision-rule about 53% of the syllabi examined (N=40) were multidisciplinary in nature.

Team Teaching

It is widely recognized that nuclear arms education is a complex subject which appropriately--perhaps inevitably--draws on the knowledge of several disciplines. As a practical matter, communication of the special knowledge of several disciplines raises fundamental pedagogical issues concerning competence of the instructor and overall coherence of the course. Organizing relevant information and insights from the scholarship of political science, physics, nuclear engineering, history, philosophy, chemistry, economics, law, sociology, art, literature, music, mathematics, international relations, medicine, atmospheric science, and public policy is a formidable task. It is likely far beyond the usual disciplinary expertise of most individuals (Harrison 1985 28).

A single course need not include everything. Nonetheless, if we wish to discuss the social and

4

political implications of nuclear weapons, we must move beyond the conventional confines of a single discipline. Organizing this information for the classroom typically requires substantial self-education of individual instructors, few of whom have acquired a broad interdisciplinary background in nuclear issues through their formal education. Even the broadest graduate curriculum this author has discovered to date does not begin to encompass the breadth of relevant perspectives described above.

Courses taught by individuals may be expected to contain a strong disciplinary bias, even if attempts are made to communicate information from additional disciplines. Competence of the instructor will therefore vary considerably with topics covered over a semester. Breadth of course coverage will be restricted by disciplinary background and success of self-education efforts. Further, the "aura of competence" or credibility of a course may be low with a single instructor, thereby reducing its attractiveness to students with diverse interests and majors (Saperstein 1983, 320).

Multiple instructors team-teaching a course may increase the competence available to students on nuclear issues. Guest speakers with special expertise may also increase competence. However, some continuity and coherence in instruction may be sacrificed (Harrison 1985, 29; Ringler 1983, 323). Students respond positively to a variety of instructors, but may find it difficult to link one lecture to another, or correlate assigned readings with many different lectures by different persons (Saperstein 1983, 321).

Thus, instructors organizing courses on nuclear issues must balance pedagogical concerns for competent instruction with the need for coherence in presentation of concepts and information. Using a team approach to gain multidisciplinary expertise may reduce cohesiveness of presentation, impairing student comprehension and integration of relevant information, and making achievement of an interdisciplinary synthesis difficult. Unless one or more members of the team make a concerted effort to integrate lectures and assigned readings throughout the semester, students may be confused, and left with major gaps in their understanding of information presented.

As expected, team-taught courses were strongly associated with a multidisciplinary approach to nuclear issues (phi-coefficient = .744, contingency coefficient = .597). Thirty-two of the forty multidisciplinary courses examined were team-taught, while thirty-three of thirty-five discipline-based courses were taught by a single instructor. Range in number of instructors for team-taught courses was 2-26, with a mean of 6 instructors. Assuming a 3 credit course meets about 40 times per semester, a mean of 6 instructors would entail a different speaker for one lecture in seven; courses at the upper range would have a new speaker every second class period. It seems unlikely that a course could be taught with such large numbers of instructors without significant loss of coherence and student comprehension.

Guest Speakers

Use of guest speakers can add variety and credibility to a course on nuclear issues, especially if the speaker is involved in the public debate over nuclear arms. However, it is difficult to control the quality of presentations made by guest speakers (Ehrlich 1983, 337), and it may be difficult to obtain speakers willing to present and defend specific positions (Saperstein 1983, 321), such as those needed to balance presentations on controversial issues.

Linking presentations of guest speakers with other lectures and to assigned readings entails many of the difficulties discussed above concerning coherence of team-taught courses. Guest speakers cannot be expected to integrate their presentations with other lectures or assigned readings they have not heard or assigned, so this task falls to those responsible for organizing the course. Left to chance, it may fail to occur as often as not.

Guest speakers were utilized in thirty-six courses examined, ranging in number from 1-45 per syllabus. An extreme case was an advanced course offered at the Air Command Staff College, Air University, Maxwell Air Force Base, in which 45 guest speakers—often 3-6 per day in all-day schedules—addressed a class of officers over a twenty-three day period in May, 1986. These persons included an impressive array of superior military officers and civilian experts, giving presentations which often contained classified information.

Because these resources are generally not available--and may not be desirable--in courses offered to civilian students in a university setting over a longer period of time, the extreme case may appropriately be excluded from this portion of the study. It is included in later portions for consideration of topics covered in the course, which were quite similar in coverage to "civilian" courses. Excluding this extreme case, the range of guest speakers was 1-19, with a mean of six guest speakers in thirty-five courses.

Guest speakers were utilized more often in team-taught courses than in those offered by individuals. About 74% of the team-taught courses used guest speakers, while 27% of courses taught by individuals invited guest speakers. Summing the number of instructors and guests, the range of total speakers addressing forty -five courses was 2-46. Again excluding the extreme case discussed above, the range of total speakers was 2-29, with a mean of 11 speakers in forty-four courses.

Again assuming a 3-credit course meets about 40 times per semester, a mean of 11 speakers would entail a different speaker for one lecture in four; courses at the upper range would have a new speaker every second class period. Both the mean and the upper range of total speakers were considerably larger for team-taught courses. Thus, guest speakers were often used in addition to, rather than instead of the team approach. In view of these large numbers of total speakers, would it be surprising if students--and perhaps some faculty participating in such a course--began to wonder who was responsible for course content and coherence?

Frequent use of guest speakers seems likely to have sacrificed some continuity and coherence in instruction in several courses. Instructors organizing courses on nuclear arms must be cognizant of the trade-offs between the need for variety and expertise, on one hand, and the need for coherence and integration of course content, on the other hand, when deciding how many persons will address the class. A large number of speakers may make student learning more difficult, rather than facilitate it.

Required Readings

A bibliography of over 800 references to required readings and films used in these courses may be found in Chapter 4. It is of considerable interest, as there appears to be little agreement on choice of readings for classroom use among faculty teaching these courses.

Only thirteen references appeared in five or more of the syllabi examined. Half of these were general texts (Ground Zero, Inc. 1983; Harvard Nuclear Study Group 1983; Kegley and Wittkoph 1985; Mandelbaum 1979; Sivard 1983), including one by Jonathan Schell (1982) which was used in 14 of 75 courses. Although forty courses examined were interdisciplinary or multidisciplinary in nature, no general text with a science/technology and society approach was used in more than three of them.

Other texts which appeared in more than five syllabi, listed with the topic for which they were most often assigned, include: Strategic Doctrine (Forsberg, 1982); Arms Control (Blacker and Duffy, 1984); European Security (Bundy, Kennan, McNamara, and Smith 1982); History of Nuclear Weapons Development (Hersey, 1959); Effects of Nuclear Weapons (Glasstone and Dolan, 1977, Lewis 1979); Nuclear Ethics (US Catholic Bishops, 1983).

Films/Videos

Films or other audiovisual aids were used in thirty-one courses (41%). Examination of joint frequency distributions revealed no significant relationship between use of films and either a multidisciplinary approach or team-taught courses. However, weak but significant relationships were evident between use of audiovisual aids and coverage of two topics discussed below concerning nuclear physics and effects of nuclear weapons. A list of films used may be found at the end of Chapter 4.

TOPICS IN NUCLEAR EDUCATION

Harrison (1985, 27) states that University faculty tend to emphasize technological, strategic and historic factors of the nuclear arms race over moral responsibility and political choice. To test Harrison's hypothesis, course syllabi were examined to see what topics were covered most frequently. Topics were identified as described in syllabi topic headings and associated titles of required readings, then coded in twenty-four categories on the basis of synonymous terms and meanings of phrases. All coding was done by the author, who is familiar with the literature and terminology of nuclear weapons and arms control.

The number of syllabi and percentage of the sample in which each topic appeared are shown in rank order of frequency in Table 2. Because it was not possible in

TABLE 2

Topics Covered: Frequency and Percentage of Total
N=75

	N	%
Strategic Doctrine	62	(83)
Nuclear Weapons Systems	57	(76)
Arms Control	56	(75)
Arms Race	54	(72)
Effects of Nuclear Weapons	47	(63)
Nature of Threat	47	(63)
Nuclear History	47	(63)
Nuclear Ethics	45	(60)
International Relations Theory	40	(53)
Defensive Systems	39	(52)
Conflict Management	34	(45)
Nuclear Proliferation	27	(36)
Cold War	26	(35)
Nuclear Physics	25	(33)
European Security	25	(33)
Force Comparisons	21	(28)
Conventional Weapons Systems	20	(27)
Cultural Context	19	(25)
Art, Music and Literature	17	(23)
Command/Communication/Control/Intelligence	16	(21)
Intervention	14	(19)
Chemical and Biological Warfare	6	(8)
Military Service	4	(5)
Terrorism	1	(1)

all cases to discern how many class periods were devoted to a topic, a syllabus was counted only once for each topic covered.

Micro-analysis of faculty emphasis on one topic or another would require administration of a detailed questionnaire or content analysis of actual lectures, both of which were beyond the means available for this study. Thus, a less sophisticated but more convenient macro-analysis of emphasis on topics was performed by coding a nominal level variable for the threshold question of whether or not a topic was covered in a particular course.

Twenty topics were designated before coding began; four were added during coding to accommodate unexpected topics (Intervention in Foreign States, Chemical and Biological Warfare, Cultural Context of Nuclear Weapons, and Military Service). Because coding was performed on the basis of terms and phrases which may not have universally accepted meanings, precise distinctions between some cases were not possible. A sense of topic content may be had by reference to descriptions of each subject grouping in the bibliography in Chapter 4.

No topic was addressed in all of the courses examined. It was somewhat surprising to find that discussions of Nuclear Physics appeared in only one-third of the syllabi. Student understanding of topics on Nuclear Weapons Systems and Effects of Nuclear Weapons would likely be enhanced by even a rudimentary scientific explanation of physical processes of nuclear fission and fusion. Nuclear science appeared to take a back-seat role to nuclear technology in the courses examined.

On the other hand, it is interesting to note the high number of courses which addressed Effects of Nuclear Weapons, including discussions of physical, biological, atmospheric, psychological, environmental and other health effects of exploding or stockpiling nuclear weapons. Prior to recent efforts by Physicians for Social Responsibility (1982) and the TTAPS Group (Sagan, 1983/84), much of the sparse literature on these effects focused on single explosions, or was too technical to be accessible to an undergraduate or general audience.

Although recent published materials make occasional brief excursions into the arcane realm of global computer-assisted atmospheric simulation modeling, they are generally more accessible than previous curriculum materials and have the virtue of directing attention to aggregate effects of multiple warhead explosions on humankind, rather than to single explosions. Further, debate over the accuracy of these studies (Thompson and Schneider, 1986) provides a convenient illustration for students of difficulties faced by official decision makers when scientists disagree about pertinent facts and their significance.

The only topic which did not receive explicit coverage as expected was Terrorism, which appeared in only one syllabus. This was surprising, given the attention accorded this topic in contemporary courses on international relations and national security, and recent concern for theft of nuclear materials.

Terrorism with nuclear materials would not require a capability to generate a fission explosion, but only an ability to disperse toxic or radioactive materials in a human population, perhaps through drinking water, food, or drugstore medicines. However, syllabus headings and required reading titles may not have revealed treatment of this subject under another topic such as Nuclear Proliferation. At any rate, the political implications of very small scale hostile applications of nuclear materials appeared to receive infrequent treatment in courses examined.

In coverage and sequence of topics, six syllabi revealed a striking resemblance to each other, and to an article by Dietrich Schroeer (1983) about teaching nuclear issues. This suggests university faculty have looked to the literature for models when designing their own courses on nuclear technology, and that this literature, while sparse, may be expected to influence choice of topics. These were the only courses in the sample which included discussion of Chemical and Biological Warfare. No other clear pattern of duplication in coverage and sequence of topics was evident in the syllabi examined.

Three courses in military science offered at the National Defense University, the Air University at Maxwell Air Force Base, and the Naval Postgraduate School, and one political science course taught at the Air Force Academy were included in the sample for comparison with courses taught in civilian universities. Although there were significant differences in number of speakers used between courses offered in civilian universities and one military science course, discussed

11

above, the topical coverage of these courses was generally similar to others in the sample. While none of these four courses included any of the last six topics listed in Table 2, this was also true of many other courses. Two of these courses included treatment of Effects of Nuclear Weapons and Nuclear Proliferation. Three included Nuclear Ethics, using required readings similar to other courses. Minor differences included use of specially prepared military texts (in addition to commercially published materials), less use of films, and generally more voluminous reading assignments in the military science courses.

Overall, disciplinary contributions were spread broadly across the natural and social sciences, but less broadly across the humanities, where they were primarily in English, philosophy and religion. The perspectives and special insights of Art, Literature and Music, so often important sources of social criticism, were evident in only about 23% of the courses examined.

Technological, Strategic and Historical Factors

Several topics provided substantial coverage of technological factors concerning nuclear issues, including Nuclear Weapons Systems, Arms Race, Defensive Systems, Force Comparisons, Command, Control, Communications and Intelligence (C3I), Nuclear Proliferation, European Security, Conventional Weapons, and Chemical and Biological Warfare. Thus, nine of twenty-four topics (including three of ten topics covered in 50% or more of syllabi examined) included substantial treatment of technological factors.

Because many of these topics included discussion of political, economic, methodological, or management issues, and because boundaries between some topics were imprecise, it seemed desirable to simplify the analysis by identifying one or two key indicators for each factor identified by Harrison. This was accomplished by adopting a decision-rule that the "best" topic indicator for a factor identified by Harrison would be one which (a) included as its central focus issues most characteristic of that factor, and which (b) included the least topical overlap with other factors.

Thus, of the topics identified in Table 2, the single best indicator for technological factors was judged to be Nuclear Weapons Systems, which focused on engineering features and performance capabilities of nuclear technologies. Nuclear Weapons Systems was the second most frequently covered topic, appearing in 57 (76%) of the syllabi studied.

The best indicator for strategic factors appeared to be Strategic Doctrine, which included discussions of war planning, fighting and avoidance, with treatment of deterrence, escalation, retaliation and grand strategy. Strategic Doctrine was the most frequently addressed topic, appearing in 68 (83%) of the syllabi studied. Some peripheral discussion of strategy was also evident in topics on Nuclear Weapons Systems, Nuclear Proliferation, European Security and Defensive Systems.

The best indicator for historical factors was Nuclear History, which included discussions of the development of nuclear weapons, with reference to persons involved, motives, and their use at Hiroshima and Nagasaki. Nuclear History was the seventh most frequently covered topic, appearing in 47 (63%) of syllabi examined. Historical events were also mentioned, but were not the major emphasis under headings for Strategic Doctrine, Arms Control, Arms Race, Nature of the Threat, Conflict Management, Nuclear Physics, Nuclear Proliferation, European Security, Conventional Weapons, Cold War, Intervention in Foreign States, Cultural Context of Nuclear Weapons, and Military Service.

Thus, technological, strategic and historical factors concerning the nuclear arms race received substantial treatment in the syllabi examined for this study. But did they receive more frequent treatment than issues of moral responsibility and political choice?

Moral Responsibility and Political Choice

The best indicator for issues of moral responsibility in this study was Nuclear Ethics, which included discussions of moral, ethical and religious questions raised by use of nuclear technology. This was the eighth most frequently covered topic, appearing in 45 (60%) of syllabi examined.

Indicators for political choice were less clear cut, there being elements of political choice in several topics, including Strategic Doctrine, Arms Control, Arms Race, Nature of the Threat, Nuclear History, Conflict Management, Nuclear Proliferation, European Security, Intervention in Foreign States, and Military Service. The best indicators of political choice appear to be Arms Control and Arms Race because they concern significant numbers of observable decisions (treaties, expenditures).

Arms Control included discussions of the history, economics and politics of arms control and disarmament efforts concerning both nuclear and nonnuclear weapons, with treatment of treaty negotiations, attitudes of governments and citizens towards them, and proposals for a nuclear freeze. Arms Control was the third most frequently covered topic, appearing in 56 (75%) of the syllabi studied.

Arms Race included discussions of the history, causes, politics and economics of weapons purchases, defense spending, force development and modernization, with reference to the role of the "military-industrial complex." Arms Race was the fourth most frequently covered topic, appearing in 54 (72%) of the courses.

Simplifying this analysis greatly, the factors discussed by Harrison are described by the best indicator topics for each in Table 3. Rankings are from Table 2 above.

TABLE 3

Arms Race Factors and Indicator Topics by Rank

Factor	Indicator	Rank	N	%
Strategic Factors	Strategic Doctrine	1	62	(83)
Technological Factors	Nuclear Weapons	2	57	(76)
Political Choice	Arms Control	3	56	(75)
Political Choice	Arms Race	4	54	(72)
Historical Factors	Nuclear History	5	47	(63)
Moral Responsibility	Nuclear Ethics	8	45	(60)

In terms of frequency with which best indicator topics were addressed in the syllabi examined, Harrison's hypothesis was verified for strategic and technological factors, which receive more treatment than either moral responsibility or political choice. Contrary to the hypothesis, political choice appears to be covered nearly as often as technological factors, and more often than historical factors. Moral responsibility appears to receive less treatment than the other four factors. Perhaps more significant than which factor receives more frequent treatment is the observation that all these factors received substantial treatment in more than half of the courses examined: none appears to have been slighted.

RELATIONSHIPS

Joint frequency distributions were examined for pairs of topics and single topics with other variables. Relationships between the topic Nuclear Ethics and the approach used to teach a course are shown in Table 4. Nuclear Ethics is moderately strongly associated with a multidisciplinary approach and strongly associated with a team-teaching approach.

TABLE 4

Measures of Association for Nuclear Ethics
with Teaching Approach
N = 75

	Multi-disciplinary	Team Teaching	Multiple Speakers
Corrected Chi-square	12.556	14.708	20.891
Significance	<.0005	<.0005	<.0005
Phi-coefficient	.436	.470	.556
Contingency coeff.	.400	.425	.486
Lambda	.400*	.382**	.467

* With Nuclear Ethics dependent.
** With team-teaching dependent.

Nuclear Ethics was also associated with multiple speakers in a course, regardless of whether it is multidisciplinary or team-taught. With lambda calculated at .467, knowledge that multiple speakers address a class increases by 47% our ability to correctly guess that the topic Nuclear Ethics is discussed, when compared to guesses made with information about only the case distribution of Nuclear Ethics. This indicates a moderately strong association. Securing someone to address the moral, ethical or religious dimensions of nuclear weaponry appears to be a high priority among faculty organizing courses using multiple speakers.

Relationships between the topics Nuclear Weapons Systems, Defensive Systems, and Arms Control are shown in Table 5. Treatment of Nuclear Weapons Systems is weakly but significantly associated with discussion of Defensive Systems, which includes defensive weapons technologies (antiballistic missiles, ballistic missile defense, SDI) and management measures (civil defense, evacuation plans) developed in preparation for nuclear war. Both topics emphasize engineering features and performance capabilities of strategic nuclear weaponry. Discussion of Defensive Systems is not significantly related to any other topic or variable.

TABLE 5

Measures of Association for Nuclear Weapons Systems
with Defensive Systems and Arms Control
N = 75

	Defensive Systems	Arms Control
Corrected Chi-square	4.364	13.635
Significance	.037	<.0005
Phi-coefficient	.272	.462
Contingency coeff.	.263	.420
Lambda	.222*	.211**

* With Defensive Systems dependent.
** With Arms Control dependent.

Treatment of Nuclear Weapons Systems is moderately strongly associated with discussion of Arms Control, although the strength of association is weaker for the more conservative measure of Lambda. It may seem a bit incongruous to some readers that this association is not stronger, as nuclear arms have most often been the focus of arms control negotiations in recent times, and some familiarity with the technological capabilities of nuclear weapons may be expected to be useful in understanding the complexity of negotiations and related treaties. However, some courses focus on processes of negotiation and stress the diplomatic history of arms control over technical aspects.

Discussion of Nuclear Physics is weakly but significantly associated with treatment of International Relations Theory, use of audiovisual aids, and team-teaching, as shown in Table 6.

TABLE 6

Measures of Association for Nuclear Physics
and Three Topics
N = 75

	International Relations Theory	Film, Video	Team Teaching
Corrected Chi-square	5.632	6.605	4.203
Significance	.018	.010	.040
Phi-coefficient	.302	.325	.265
Contingency coeff.	.289	.310	.256
Lambda*	.257*	.226**	.206***

* With International Relations Theory dependent.
** With Film/Video dependent.
*** With team-teaching dependent.

Team-teaching is also weakly associated with treatment of Arms Control (phi-coefficient = .346) and the Cold War (phi-coefficient = .350). Discussion of Conventional (nonnuclear) Weapons Systems is similarly associated with multiple speakers (phi-coefficient = .308). These weak associations seem to underscore the use of team-teaching to secure greater competence of instruction in areas which may be beyond the expertise of a single instructor.

Table 7 shows measures of association for the topic International Relations Theory with Effects of Nuclear Weapons, Nature of the Threat, and Nuclear History. International Relations Theory is weakly but significantly associated with all three of these topics, none of which is significantly related to the others.

TABLE 7

Measures of Association for
International Relations Theory and Three Topics
N = 75

	Effects of Nuclear Weapons	Nature of the Threat	Nuclear History
Corrected Chi-square	4.775	4.500	4.775
Significance	.029	.034	.029
Phi-coefficient	.280	.273	.280
Contingency coeff.	.270	.263	.270
Lambda*	.200	.229	.200

* With International Relations Theory dependent.

Discussions of International Relations Theory include theories of political, economic and social change, dependence and interdependence, conflict, aggression, cooperation, balance of power, national power, coercion, war, alliances, foreign and national security policy making, cultural and economic imperialism, and containment. Recalling that 27% of the syllabi examined were political science courses, it seems likely these relationships are at least partly attributes of historical and conceptual orientations of that discipline.

For example, balance of power theory can hardly be made intelligible without reference to competing nation-states, and their perceptions and attitudes toward each other: which define the nature of the threat. Descriptions of the biological, atmospheric, psychological, and other environmental health effects of nuclear weapons may be deemed useful in dramatizing the severity of the threat. That such discussions in courses on nuclear arms would be placed in historical context of the development and use of nuclear weapons hardly seems surprising. At any rate, there appears to be some clustering of topics in 53% of the sample in which International Relations Theory appeared.

Treatment of Effects of Nuclear Weapons is also weakly but significantly associated with use of audio-visual aids such as films and videos (phi-coefficient = .368) and multiple speakers (phi-coefficient .308). Recent releases of dramatic visual representations of nuclear war, the public debate over "nuclear winter," and improved availability of lecturers with medical backgrounds to speak about health effects of nuclear weapons may help explain these relationships.

The only other significant relationship found concerned a weak association between discussions of European Security and Force Comparisons (phi-coefficient = .378). Apparently faculty teaching courses in which the nuclear dimensions of European security are singled out for special treatment (about one-third of the sample) also tend to examine methods for measuring and comparing nuclear and conventional forces of adversaries (about 28% of syllabi examined).

In spite of numerous weak associations, factor analysis failed to produce clustering of these topics into coherent composite topics. What little covariation does exist in discussion of the various topics does not appear to be interpretable by reference to a smaller number of underlying concerns. Rather, diversity of approaches and values attached to different aspects of nuclear education seem to best explain the diversity of topics covered in these courses, beyond the ten topics in Table 2 which appeared in 50% or more of courses examined.

CONCLUSIONS

Multidisciplinary courses on nuclear issues tend to be team-taught, sometimes involving substantial numbers of instructors and guest speakers. It seems likely some continuity and coherence are sacrificed in courses involving numbers of instructors and guest speakers in the upper range of those examined here, but it is beyond the scope of this study to determine whether gains in competence or credibility offset these losses. This is a matter which deserves careful consideration by faculty responsible for organizing such courses.

As expected, technological, strategic and historical factors concerning the nuclear arms race received substantial emphasis in the syllabi examined. Moral responsibility and political choice received more emphasis than expected, with more frequent treatment than historical factors. Discussions of moral responsibility are associated with use of a multidisciplinary approach, team teaching, and use of guest speakers.

It was somewhat encouraging to find that technological factors did not appear to dominate the teaching of courses on nuclear weapons, although individual courses may exhibit such a bias. As a group, the courses examined appear to present a mix of decision-relevant information concerning technological and social issues, often in historical context with consideration of moral responsibility for national policy choices. It seems likely the public debate which is necessary to democratic decision making will be better informed and expanded if technological dimensions of nuclear weapons are demystified and made accessible to the citizenry through discussion of their strategic implications, political significance, and moral ramifications.

But circumstances change. Barring sudden reversal of recent developments, we may soon find ourselves in a situation where arms control negotiations take a less prominent role in our relations with the Soviet Union than pollution control negotiations driven by global atmospheric change. We may find that nuclear weapons are of greater concern in our relations with our allies, and with any number of Third World nations and terrorist groups, than with the Soviet Union.

Many of the courses examined in this study appear to have been shaped significantly by recent public debates concerning defensive weapons systems and global effects of multiple nuclear detonations. Whether these courses will continue to be taught, and the success of efforts to adapt them to changing circumstances if we move into a relationship of decreased tensions with the Soviet Union, are subjects for future research.

NOTES

(1) Colleges and Universities with nuclear education courses included in this study were: Air Force Academy, Air University at Maxwell AFB, American University, Berkshire Community College, Boise State University, Boston University, University of California, Berkeley, University of California, Davis, University of California, Irvine, University of California, San Diego, University of Chicago, Colgate University, Clark University, University of Colorado, Columbia University, Dartmouth Medical School, Davidson College, Denver University, DePaul University, Drury University, Duke University, Emory University, Florida State University, University of Georgia, Grinnel College, Harvard/M.I.T. Summer Program, Hobart and William Smith Colleges, Lafayette College, George Mason University, University of Massachusetts-Boston, University of Maryland, Metropolitan State College (Denver), Michigan State University, University of Minnesota, Massachusetts Institute of Technology, Mount Holyoke College, National Defense University, Naval Postgraduate School, New York University, University of North Carolina, University of North Dakota, Notre Dame, Ohio State University, Princeton University, Rancho Santiago College, San Diego State University, University of Southern California, University of Southern Maine, Stanford University, SUNY-Cortland, SUNY-Purchase, SUNY-Stony Brook, Temple University, Texas A & M, Tulane University, Washington State University, Williams College, University of Wisconsin-Madison, Yale University.

REFERENCES

Alexander, Susan, ed. 1984. **Bibliography of Nuclear Education resources 1984**. Cambridge, MA: Educators for Social Responsibility.

Blacker, Coit, and Gloria Duffy, eds. 1984. **International Arms Control: Issues and Agreements**, 2d ed. Palo Alto, CA: Stanford University Press.

Bulletin of the Atomic Scientists. 1984. "Nuclear War: A Teaching Guide." 40: 1s-32s.

Bundy, McGeorge, George F. Kennan, Robert McNamara, and Gerard Smith. 1982. "Nuclear Weapons and the Atlantic Alliance." Foreign Affairs 60: 753-68.

Durch, William J. 1983. "The Nuclear Age: A Course Description." J. of College Science Teaching 12: 330-32.

Ehrlich, Robert. 1983. "Nuclear War: An Interdisciplinary Course at George Mason University." J. of College Science Teaching 12: 336-37.

_____. 1987. Proceedings of the Second George Mason University Nuclear War and Peace Education Conference, October 29-31, 1987. Fairfax, VA: George Mason University.

Federation of American Scientists. 1984. FAS Syllabus Packet. Washington, DC: Federation of American Scientists.

Forsberg, Randall. 1982. "A Bilateral Nuclear Weapons Freeze." Scientific American, November. Offprint #744.

Glasstone, S., and A. Dolan. 1977. Effects of Nuclear Weapons, 3d ed. Washington, DC: Government Printing Office.

Ground Zero, Inc. 1983. [Roger Molander]. Nuclear War: What's In It for You? New York: Ground Zero/Pocket Books.

Hahn, Carole L. 1985. "The Status of Nuclear Education in Social Studies: Report of a Survey." The Social Studies 76: 247-53.

Hamilton, Michael S. 1989. "Multidisciplinary Teaching About Nuclear Arms." J. of College Science Teaching. 58 (March/April): 318-23.

Harrison, Michael J. 1985. "Teaching Undergraduates About Nuclear Arms and Strategy." J. of College Science Teaching 15: 26-30.

Harvard Educational Review. 1984. "Education and the Threat of Nuclear War." 54: Special Issue.

Teaching About Nuclear Arms

Harvard Nuclear Study Group. 1983. *Living With Nuclear Weapons*. New York: Bantam Books.

Hersey, John. 1959. *Hiroshima*. New York: Bantam Books.

J. of College Science Teaching. 1983. "Nuclear Education." 12: Special Issue.

Kegley, Charles W., and Eugene R. Wittkoph, eds. *The Nuclear Reader: Strategy, Weapons, War*. New York: St. Martin's, 1985.

Kohn, Walter, and Lawrence Badash. 1988. *The University and the Nuclear Predicament*. San Diego: University of California Institute on Global Conflict and Cooperation.

Lewis, Kevin. 1979. "The Prompt and Delayed Effects of Nuclear War." *Scientific American*. 241 (July): 35-47.

Mandelbaum, Michael. 1979. *The Nuclear Question: The United States and Nuclear Weapons 1946-1976*. New York: Cambridge University Press.

Physicians for Social Responsibility. 1982. *Preparing for Nuclear War: The Psychological Effects*. New York: Physicians for Social Responsibility.

Physics Today. 1983. "Nuclear Arms Education." 36: Special Issue.

Ringler, Dick. 1983. "The University of Wisconsin-Madison's Perspectives on Nuclear War: Goals, Organization and Structure." *J. of College Science Teaching* 12: 322-25.

Sagan, Carl. 1983/84. "Nuclear War and Climatic Catastrophe: Some Policy Implications." *Foreign Affairs* 62 (Winter): 257-292.

Saperstein, Alvin M. 1983. "Nuclear War: An Interdisciplinary Undergraduate Course." *J. of College Science Teaching* 12: 319-21.

Schell, Jonathan. 1982. *The Fate of the Earth*. New York: Knopf.

Schroeer, Dietrich. 1983. "Teaching on Science, Technology and the Nuclear Arms Race." J. of College Science Teaching 12: 310-14.

Sivard, Ruth. 1983. World Military and Social Expenditures, 1983. Leesburg, VA: World Priorities.

Teaching Political Science. 1987. "A Symposium on Security Studies," edited by Stephen F. Szabo. 14: 108-44.

Thompson, Starley L., and Stephen H. Schneider. 1986. Foreign Affairs 64 (Summer): 981-1005.

United Campuses to Prevent Nuclear War. 1984. Summary of Courses on Nuclear War. Washington, DC: United Campuses to Prevent Nuclear War.

US Catholic Bishops. 1983. "The Challenge of Peace: God's Promise and Our Response." Origins. May 19.

Wein, Barbara, ed. 1987. Peace and World Order Studies: A Curriculum Guide, 5th ed. New York: World Policy Institute.

Winder, Alvin E., and Mary Anne Stanitis. 1988. "Nuclear Education in Public Health and Nursing." American Journal of Public Health 78 (August): 967-68.

CHAPTER 2:   THE POLITICAL CORE OF NUCLEAR WEAPONS TEACHING

William A. Lindeke

University of Lowell

Political science courses on nuclear weapons and arms control have often focused on the dynamic between technical approaches and political ones. Some courses emphasize the technology of nuclear weapons and complex strategic doctrines associated with them. In others, political dimensions are mostly associated with national security policy, arms control negotiations and international relations.

In recent years there has been a rapid proliferation of new materials and approaches to accompany a similar expansion of student interest and course offerings in this area. Part of this growth is related to the technologies and strategic concerns associated with first strike weapons and defensive options. In addition, this growth reflects increased concerns and fears of common citizens and students about the threat of nuclear war.

The important questions for teachers of political science then become: What are the issues of greatest relevance to everyday life?   How should they be portrayed in the classroom?

Fortunately, the explosion of relevant literature allows an expanded menu of items and approaches for classroom consideration. Some courses focus on strategic policy and its relationship to the unprecedented character of atomic and nuclear factors in the military equation.   Many early strategic theorists like Schelling, Wohlstetter and Kahn were scientists, engineers and mathematicians who gave a strong technical orientation to the field.   Similarly, writers and teachers in this area represent institutions inside the strategic policy-making loop, giving them a narrower range of pedagogical interests (e.g., Teaching Political Science 1987).   Some recent additions to the field emphasize ethical issues and consequences of the use of nuclear weapons.   Declarations of the Catholic

Bishops' Conference (in Harris and Markusen 1986) and Jonathon Schell's popular <u>Fate of the Earth</u>, for example, have stimulated new areas of concern. Thus, a more political focus is apparent (1) in many newer contributions to the field.

This chapter reflects course content I developed over five years of teaching a course titled "Defense and Disarmament" at the University of Lowell. During that time, I encouraged students to acquire detailed knowledge of different weapon systems and the strategic nomenclature required to plow through the national security literature. Yet, I continue to rely mostly on basic concepts of political analysis to work through the issues. It is my belief that explanation of this complex subject matter in our classrooms gains a great deal from an ordinary political science approach (2).

That is, in addition to complicated arguments about strategy and advanced technologies, national security issues are often about very ordinary political themes. For instance, they deal with ideology, culture, and socialization that form the individual's basic orientation toward other countries.

Further, conflict among interests in society is central to all aspects of security studies. Various groups contend for power and to maximize their advantage through government policy, whether those group interests are geographical, partisan, class, industrial, bureaucratic or organizational. The state and its myriad components have specific interests and the power to assert and defend them against both domestic and foreign rivals. The state thus plays an active part in whatever social conflict ensues, including intrastate battles such as those between the military services. The policy process that results from this political environment deserves expanded attention in our classrooms, along with technical and military issues. The following discussion illustrates how some of these political themes are usefully incorporated into teaching about nuclear issues.

POLITICAL CONTENT: WHO CONTROLS THE DEBATE?

National security debates are often over who gets to participate in decision-making and framing the issues. Therefore, one of my starting points for political science courses is analysis of the interests and points of view of the participants in foreign and nuclear policy making.

This approach can be illustrated by reference to the Harvard University Nuclear Study Group's text <u>Living With Nuclear Weapons</u> (1983), which brought together diverse scholars in an attempt to recapture a guiding role for experts in the US nuclear debate. Their quest for control of the issues crossed academic, policy and political boundaries. Their efforts were in part a response to the Nuclear Freeze Movement and other citizen-activist opponents of nuclear weapons buildup, who constituted the political challengers to official policy. In the late 1970's efforts by a more hawkish group, the Committee on the Present Danger (Wolfe 1979; Scheer 1982), constituted a similar attempt to restore a different set of experts to positions of power that define the issues.

Despite the technical and sometimes Byzantine character of national security discussions, they are essentially dominated by viewpoints which are deeply held. John Kenneth Galbraith, among others, points to the "deeply theological" nature of arms control and national security issues. (3) Thus, as an integral part of national security studies I encourage students to look for underlying values and interests of participants in security discussions. Debates in the national security area are no less ideological than in other areas that students and faculty analyze. Such analysis facilitates the students' critical evaluation of policy alternatives.

Daniel Yergin (1977), George Kennan, Michael Nacht and others provide evidence for the enduring character and the <u>a priori</u> nature of American policy elites' attitudes toward the Soviet Union and the intentions of its leadership. Yergin argues that debates focusing on the Soviet Union are in large measure predetermined by long-standing attitudes toward that state as an adversary requiring national security responses, and that they are not the result of changes in technical details of Soviet force structure or specific actions. A recent study of public opinion finds a similar polarization in the population as a whole (National Public Radio 1987). Hawks, doves, owls and the rest of the aviary have established programmatic or ideological positions that are minimally affected by day to day changes in personnel, policies or deployments. The two dominant positions are those who favor arms control and those who favor military buildups as the major emphasis of national security policy.

Advocates of the necessity of arms control include retired military leaders like Admiral Gene LaRoque (Dellums 1983) and nuclear scientists from the Manhattan Project like Victor Weiskopf (1987). The essential viewpoint of this group is that Soviet leaders act like those of other states in their foreign relations. On the whole they see Soviet policy as being based upon national interest, characterized by a cautious, defensive attitude. It follows from this view that arms control and diplomacy are possible and desirable as the fundamental course for US-Soviet relations.

Just as adamant on the absolute necessity for US military strength and nuclear buildup to prevent Soviet domination are other defense experts, including important officials in the Reagan Administration. Led by former Secretary of Defense Weinberger and his assistant Richard Perle, they successfully fought off arms control agreements for nearly seven years. In the perspective of this group, the Soviet Union is bound for world domination and must always be countered with military power (hence, the slogan "Peace Through Strength"). The combination of imputed expansionist intentions of Soviet leaders with particular qualitative and quantitative developments of nuclear forces worries adherents of this perspective. Richard Pipes points to enduring aspects of Russian history for the causes of this expansionism, while others emphasize rigid aims of Soviet ideology which are said to require a strong military response by the West. (4)

In the classroom, then, understanding of these orientations can be the starting point for a demystification of the dense technical complexity which often dominates public debate about nuclear forces. That is to say, we begin with a healthy skepticism about security issues and ask to what extent it is new details or prior assumptions that lead to answers given by the experts. Similarly, development of this critical attitude should also help to demystify the emotionally charged "threat inflation" which typifies so much of the discussion from all sides. It may also help to deal with problems of secrecy and manipulation of information that permeate so many recent events and

The Political Core

impede our understanding (Manhoff 1984). Because these worldviews are so important to numerous related political issues (budgets, interventions, conscription, trade, elections), they are especially relevant in national security courses.

The history and determinants of conflict between the superpowers constitute important political background for students' understanding of the nuclear dilemma. How does the nuclear age differ in this respect from other periods of big power rivalry? Ideology, as I have just suggested, is an important component of the current conflict which makes it different from those of past ages.

There is also interesting new material which invites comparisons and contrasts with other rivalries. Charles Lamb (1989) provides a long historical comparison of common ideas concerning defense, arms control and disarmament from prior ages. This enables students to focus on abstract issues outside the immediate political context. Other scholars have focussed on ancient Greek rivalries between Athens and Sparta for analogies to current policies. This historical perspective can either substitute for or supplement game theory and similar approaches which help build skills among students from different academic backgrounds.

ARMS CONTROL

In addition to these overall orientations, my students consider some major features in the politics of arms control over the past forty years to understand how these views are relevant to actual policy. We now have the benefit of numerous narratives, memoirs and official transcripts from several rounds of arms control negotiations. Simulated negotiation games, role-playing exercises and computer programs are also available for classroom use. Still, students need to recognize and evaluate other agendas that occur within the context of such negotiations.

Posturing and Public Opinion

The arms control process was marked from the beginning of the atomic age by routine posturing. Offers such as the Baruch Plan, and others up to the present have often been promoted in the certainty that they would be rejected by the other party (Schloming 1987, 111). Despite often dramatic rhetoric of statesmen and politicians, as one analyst sees it "arms control negotiations periodically rise and fall in the favor of both the superpowers" (Blacker and Duffy 1984, 33).

At times the purpose of arms control negotiations is seemingly to maintain the process of superpower dialog; at others only to keep up appearances. Rarely has the goal on both sides been to actually reach agreements. Domestic and other agendas often are more important in the process than agreements. Alva Myrdal, Nobel Peace Prize winner in 1983, describes a permanent "game" of disarmament between the superpowers that evades serious agreements (Myrdal 1982). According to her analysis, the United States pursues technical advantages which activate Soviet insecurities; these insecurities lead them to counter with numerical buildups that raise US anxieties, which in turn lead to counteracting technical advances. In this way the superpowers avoid making changes in the basic dynamic that drives the arms race.

Albert Carnasale recently leant credence to this view with a new study at Harvard University (National Public Radio, 1986) of arms agreements conducted for the US Arms Control and Disarmament Agency (ACDA). He found that previous agreements remained within the existing force structure and modernization plans for both sides, altering little.

Often, then, one goal of negotiation is to influence public opinion at home or abroad. A recurrent scenario involves attempts to split the Atlantic Alliance or to maintain its unity, depending upon the source of the proposal. Political scientists, who are quite adept at analyzing media image making and public relations in electoral politics, can also use security issues to illustrate these processes. Students can readily follow such events and analyze them more easily than they can the technical dimensions of weapons development, or other aspects that may be shrouded in the secrecy of classified material.

In the last decade, for example, the Soviets have directed their attention to public opinion in different ways (Gottemoeller 1986). Earlier, under Khrushchev, their primary focus was to make general propaganda gains or to influence audiences in the emerging Third

World.   Indeed, Khrushchev was a master at getting mileage out of propaganda and bluff. Ultimately it led to his downfall, following his failure in the Cuban Missile Crisis. By contrast, Brezhnev influenced public opinion to create favorable arms control outcomes.

These efforts, introduced in the 1970's, have increased and become more sophisticated under General Secretary Gorbachev, but the orientation seems the same.   They are directed primarily at Western audiences, but are also occasionally for Soviet domestic consumption.   These developments are challenging for American political leaders. However, the openness and direct approach are welcome, if still limited, changes in Soviet conduct.   Again, this is an ordinary political process that is quite well understood in different contexts, and may be usefully employed by faculty with students in security-related courses.

Building National Power

As   the   Reagan   Administration   affected   its "breakout" from the limits of the SALT II Treaty at the end of 1986, it also threatened to undermine other "treaty regimes" such as SALT I and, most importantly, the Antiballistic Missile Treaty (ABM).   Arms buildups were preferred over treaties early in this administration.   The Strategic Defense Initiative (or Star Wars) remained a favored program of President Reagan, and its introduction shifted much of the subsequent debate over strategy to putatively defensive approaches. (5)

However, a strong underlying purpose for the Reagan Administration, as for many previous administrations was apparently to pursue other political ends through military buildup.   In this view a stronger military (meaning more weapons and a more willing and aggressive use of them) are seen as useful in attaining cooperation or acceptance in a variety of international conflicts and arenas.   There are also domestic political gains that result from a permanent crisis, such as the Cold War, which many presidents have used to advantage.

Enhancing Domestic Power

One of the consequences of having external enemies in international relations is easier justification of centralization of domestic power and authority. By emphasizing crisis abroad, a leader may benefit at home. President Carter, for instance, was able to secure Congressional approval, under pretext of foreign crisis, for a military draft registration system that probably could not have been achieved otherwise. In delivering "evil empire" speeches and making exaggerated claims to Soviet military superiority, the Reagan Administration, perhaps more than its predecessors, promoted its political power and other domestic and international agendas.

In teaching about these issues, we need to ask students to analyze political motivations and anticipate potential consequences, in addition to learning technological details. Realistically, such an emphasis may also be more within the reach of many students, given their diverse backgrounds and skills. For example, the timing and legislative strategy surrounding key issues like budgets or new weapons system procurements can usefully be examined in this larger context. Extensive published research on the effects of crises on presidential standing in public opinion polls is also relevant for students in this context.

Shifting Rhetoric, Symbols and Problem Definition

During the past decade, proliferation of political rhetoric such as "war-winning," "prevailing," "peace through strength," "limited and prolonged nuclear war" and similar terms has drastically shifted the official debate over American nuclear thinking. The reactionary viewpoint of the Committee on the Present Danger (including many disgruntled former liberals) came to dominate official thought and is even considered moderate in some news media. Developments that have brought war-fighting mentality to the fore have also elicited higher levels of personal and collective anxiety (Mack 1983; Kovel 1983). Massive public response has brought the security debate to the streets of Europe and America, as well as into ballot boxes and legislative arenas which are amenable to analysis by students.

Euromissile deployments, and the resulting breakdown of the Intermediate-range Nuclear Force (INF) talks, are one case in point. In this instance, the technical factor of a very short flight time for highly accurate Pershing II missiles to Soviet command and control centers exacerbated political conflict between

The Political Core

the superpowers, and heightened public concerns in both
Europe and America. Later successful negotiation of
the INF Treaty is thus a dramatic indicator of reduced
tensions, which may catalyze serious efforts at negotiating other issues such as reductions in conventional
forces in Europe.

The possibility of preemptive attacks against
new, incomplete deployments, especially against Star
Wars technologies, presents another ominous future
threat. Both superpowers perceive this "defensive"
technology as threatening if first acquired by the other side, and may find strong incentives to risk preventing its deployment, especially if this can be done
in space with little or no loss of human life. Again,
students readily perceive the dynamic between technical
factors and political ones in this case.

Hegemony

Projection of American and Soviet power through
military buildup is directed toward nonnuclear states
as well. Some hard-line American advisors seek a
military capacity sufficient to force the Soviets into
conceding political hegemony to the US. These advisors
prefer conditions at least comparable to those of the
1950's, and some perhaps seek to realize the wildest
fantasies of the "rollback" advocates of that era.
That is one possible hidden agenda of recent military
policy and arms control discussions.

Economic Drain

Since Gorbachev's elevation to leadership, the
Soviet Union has seemed sincere in its desire to remove
the burden of massive expenditures for strategic arms,
in order to achieve economic improvements. This claim
is plausible because it appears to be in their own interest. It has been an enduring motive for arms control by the Soviets, going back to Salt I and ABM
(Blacker and Duffy, 49). They have seen only minor
successes in recent nonmilitary modernization efforts,
such as increased work discipline, anti-alcoholism and
decentralized management responsibility. Further advances in economic reform seem tied to reductions in
military spending.

Continued military buildup could cause further
deterioration in the Soviet economy. Some American

leaders would prefer to keep this pressure on the Soviet economy rather than reach arms control agreements. As President, Ronald Reagan indicated his opposition to earlier treaties, based on his belief that the Soviets used negotiations to gain time, or as a subterfuge for future increases to pursue their permanent aggressive agenda (Blacker 1987,134). Of course, this view shifted dramatically with his signing of the INF Treaty.

Consequently, the Soviet leadership has, in both words and deeds, appeared more willing to alter its previous positions to achieve some measure of arms reduction. This is reflected in dramatic shifts in Soviet negotiating positions on issues such as the INF Treaty, nuclear test bans, chemical weapons, and on-site inspections. These examples provide excellent opportunities to move classroom discussion beyond "evil empire" simplicities to broader political issues behind the negotiations.

PSYCHOLOGICAL FACTORS AND THE ROBUSTNESS OF DETERRENCE

In examining military policy during the last decade, several political themes recur. In substantially all past election year allegations of pending US inferiority (spending gaps, a window of vulnerability, a civil defense gap, to name a few), the argument has not been that weapons would actually be used, but that the other side would gain some psychological or political advantage from the appearance of an imbalance in power (Gaddis 1982, 36). Frequent testimony of Paul Nitze on a perceived, but perhaps not real "window of vulnerability" should be sufficient evidence of this political tactic (Fallows 1982).

Repeated claims of threat inflators, that the Soviets are about to make a major breakthrough which will put the West at some ominous risk, ring hollow to reason and evidence but may have a powerful emotional influence on voters and key public figures for a time (Blacker 1984; Scheer 1982; Talbott 1984). Although the public repeatedly is informed of great advancements in Soviet military technology, the skeptics' case all too often is stronger. My students consider, for example, the "Foxbat" fighter, Yellow Rain, super-sized submarines, and CIA estimates of Soviet military spending, all of which proved far less threatening than originally advertised (Cockburn 1984; Fallows 1982).

34

The Political Core

Confrontations over the defense budget appear especially susceptible to manipulation of fears concerning
anticipated Soviet breakthroughs.

By contrast, political scientist Robert Jervis
makes a strong claim for the enduring vitality of
mutual second strike destruction as the fundamental
guarantor of deterrence and superpower stability
(Jervis 1984). He continues a tradition established by
Bernard Brodie, the early national security analyst.
Brodie argued that the existence and destructiveness of
nuclear weapons are determining factors in national security in the nuclear age. The robustness of deterrence
with even a small number of nuclear warheads is surely
sufficient to prevent a nuclear exchange. (6) As
Galbraith often repeats: It would be impossible to
distinguish between the rubble of capitalism and that
of socialism after a nuclear exchange.

Therefore, minor shifts in tactical advantage and
strained scenarios of first strike potential heighten
political activity and budget outcomes, but can hardly
be expected to affect the parity that comes with tens
of thousands of strategic nuclear warheads. It appears
that the desire for political advantage on both domestic and international fronts must be the primary motivation for these scenarios.

For example, the minisummit in Reykjavik, Iceland
further illustrates the durability of deterrence at
much lower levels of force posture. Although some media confusion was apparent over the exact details of
plans that were discussed, the reductions reported were
staggering compared to previous agreements, and far ex-
ceeded what the disarmament community could have hoped
for in its wildest dreams. The limited proposals of
the Freeze Movement or Alva Myrdal seem modest by comparison. Only Jonathon Schell's call for total abolition approximates those initiatives (Schell 1984).

At Reykjavik, and subsequent summits, the arms
control proposals were bold and dramatic (7). Imagine
proposing to eliminate from half to all ballistic or
nuclear weapons! The most important element in these
discussions was that for both sides there appeared some
inkling of just how much might be put up for
negotiation, and just how little is necessary for deterrence. Again, this opens up a wide range of classroom scenarios for role playing and discussion.

Nuclear Weapons in the University Classroom

Professors and students may also approach these matters fruitfully from the electoral angle (8). Well-known aspects of American electoral processes include debates over perceptions of the relative strength or weakness of various candidates' or parties' images concerning their approach to the Soviet Union and military challenges. "Wimp" is the contemporary replacement for the older term "soft" as a negative campaign label.

On the other hand, some electoral contests may well turn on the perceived need for negotiations and arms control. Interesting social-psychological aspects of these issues have been considered in part under the term "gender gap" in the 1980's, but more direct analysis would be useful within national security courses. Presidential elections regularly feature contests concerning levels of response or perceptions of response to specific weaponry or Soviet threats (e.g., the various "gaps"). Spending levels, jobs and specific weapons systems or military bases often form the basis of local electoral contests. Thus, students should be encouraged to look at the ordinary electoral dynamics involving certain defense issues.

CREDIBILITY AND COMMITMENT

Similar political issues are raised by the concern with credibility. Again, perceptions and fears of ones adversaries perceptions of strength or weakness often dominate policy discussions. For example, the decision to deploy Euromissiles turned on some European leaders' worry that the American nuclear commitment to Europe was somehow no longer credible. The result was a dual track decision to deploy a new generation of threatening missiles while pursuing discussions for bilateral reductions. Simultaneously, NATO agreed to a three percent real increase in military spending. Such concerns, where the credibility of US resolve is reputedly being tested, constitute an important political dynamic that should be examined closely to enable students to evaluate the implications of this often-used justification.

One variation of this theme recurs in the question: How much is enough? The policy response to this question evokes "worst case" scenarios that build into the Pentagon's budget and force structure a condition of multiple redundancies and overkill. "Worst case" approaches also centralize and enhance the power of the beneficiaries of this largesse.

"Enough" is not just a technical issue. It is also a political one which calls forth a variety of political determinants. Numerous cases could be cited, but the decision about how much damage capability is sufficient for deterrence is a particularly relevant one. For example, when faced with a particularly expensive option to retain a specific level of damage capability, President Eisenhower simply reduced the level necessary to qualify as adequate (Kaplan,1983). Since the days of Harry Truman, political responses to budget limitations have frequently required alterations in the final determination of what is "enough." The routine approach of Congress has been to reduce the "readiness" accounts for conventional forces to deal with budget crises. These cases provide excellent examples of the dynamic between political and technical factors, and are readily available for classroom use or student research projects.

Perhaps the most famous example of an enduring, arbitrary political decision is that of the Kennedy Administration to deploy one thousand intercontinental missiles following electoral campaign emphasis on a nonexistent missile gap. The number chosen in this case had little justification other than that some buildup was necessary to fulfill campaign promises, and one thousand seemed substantial (Kaplan 1983, 325), although far less than the 7,000-10,000 ICBMs then advocated by some in the Air Force.

A related issue arises concerning verification (Scribner 1985), where decisions are often politicized, based on non-technical factors such as trust or the likelihood of Soviet cheating. Even the issue of Soviet cheating has become politicized with moralistic condemnation by those opposed to arms control. In this case, the issue is not whether violations are militarily significant. Rather, alleged violations purportedly provide evidence of the untrustworthiness of Soviet leaders.

Similarly, treaty violations are often judged on subjective political appeals rather than exclusively objective criteria. In our teaching we should emphasize these political factors rather than treating them only as technical sounding "verification" problems.

They are political conflicts of interests, ideologies and policy approaches subject to analysis like any others.

It is important to note the dynamic between political and technical issues such as those that occur in verification. Two cases provide useful illustrations. Development of satellite technologies for verification allowed greater reliability for arms control agreements. A breakthrough in seismographic measurement capabilities allowed for discrimination between nuclear explosions and earthquakes, which facilitated the Limited Test Ban Treaty.

BUREAUCRATIC INTERESTS AT WORK

An additional example of political influence comes into play with various forms of bureaucratic politics. Here I wish only to illustrate the types of conflict that result in important decisions. This theme is strong in other areas of political science teaching, yet is often ignored in the national security area. Various research labs and consulting firms, including the so-called "beltway bandits" around Washington, DC are driven by institutional interests and self-promotion like any industrial or agricultural interest. The various bureaucracies involved in policy making and arms control negotiations constitute a rich area for study, since rivalries are the norm between Defense and State Departments, the Arms Control and Disarmament Agency, National Security Council staff and the Executive Office of the President.

Interservice rivalries over acquisition of weapons systems, their designs, missions and strategies are another major source of interest conflict (Kaplan, 1983). Indeed, the whole structure of armed service careers is now focussed on managerial behavior, as judged by the same criteria of success as private sector activity. The possibility for second careers, which so many senior officers secure with defense contractors, influences the decision process. The loyalty shown by service branches to particular defense contractors, who often provide the sole information on purported Soviet weapons capabilities, and the systematic procedure for follow-on contracting and noncompetitive procurement practices are fertile ground for political analysis (Gansler 1980; Fallows 1982).

Party political issues become involved as electioneering causes certain candidates to adopt technologies and weapons systems as campaign centerpieces (e.g., John Kennedy and ICBMs, or Jack Kemp and Star Wars). Historically, more military spending has been easier to sell to the electorate than less. Jobs that are in place in a district are more concrete than promises. Thus very few weapons systems ever get cancelled. As Speaker O'Neil was fond of saying, "All politics is local." Defense contractors, unions and veterans groups enter the election fray as powerful constituencies and active participants. In the early eighties the Freeze Movement was also active on the electoral scene. These areas constitute rich fields for instruction and student research.

There are also Republican and Democratic weapons, bases and suppliers in states and Congressional Districts that must be expanded, preserved or protected. Examples abound, such as the F-18 fighter (Massachusetts and Missouri Democrat) and the B-1 bomber (hundreds of districts and more than forty states). The porkbarrel nature of defense spending ought to be given greater attention as an explanation of particular policies, not just as an overall view of the effects of military spending on the national economy. These cases provide nearly perfect examples of interest group conflict and strategy for regular classroom use.

Finally, as James Fallows makes clear in **National Defense** (1982), a culture of procurement with a life of its own has developed to drive the nuclear and nonnuclear arms race for both superpowers. Fallows' concept facilitates an understanding of the process by which individuals, groups and institutions have their interests (jobs, profits, careers and beliefs) incorporated into the arms race so it becomes an extension of their own life choices. This seems to me a much more powerful formulation than the older idea of a "military-industrial complex." Fallows' approach is especially useful in demonstrating interrelationships in a systematic fashion.

Through this political convergence of interests, the Pentagon has amassed an enormous backlog of uncontracted budget authority that will take years to exhaust. William Kaufmann of the Brookings Institution estimates an unobligated budget authority for FY 1986 of $55.7 billion (Kaufmann 1986, 11). Congress's usual pattern of budget reduction is to stretch out the "slow money" allocations on things like weapons procurement and trim the "fast money" components like maintenance and repair, rather than cut whole programs. Although budget increases have slowed or halted in recent years, the Pentagon's prospects for the near future seem bright under any of the likely budget scenarios. The richness of materials on the economic impact of defense spending and Fallow's concept of culture of procurement ensure that this approach will remain a major subject for classroom analysis.

In a democracy, it is essential that students be shown citizens need not turn over momentous decisions on seemingly complex technical subjects to an expert elite, who may not share or emphasize the same values as the surrounding society. Nuclear issues are much too important to be left to experts. Such persons may be useful to society, but theirs is the burden of persuasion, hopefully on grounds other than mere appeal to authority (e.g., their own expertise).

I have indicated some ordinary political concepts which I have found useful in addressing nuclear issues in classes on Defense and Disarmament. The special knowledge and insights of political science provide a solid foundation for accessing, understanding, evaluating and ultimately changing unacceptable social circumstances. Therein lies our strength and our hopes and the basis for our teaching.

NOTES

1. By "political" I mean that the issues involve conflict over power and control within the older questions of who gets what and why they get it. The classic statement of this view of politics was articulated by a student of symbolism and human motivation in national security studies, Harold Lasswell (1950).

2. See the excellent collections of specialized political science readings in Kegley and Wittkopf (1985), Harris and Markusen (1986), and Miller (1984). New texts that cover major issues from a variety of viewpoints which are particularly suited to the classroom approach advocated in this chapter include Schloming (1987) and (Lamb) 1988.

3.   Galbraith suggests there are two forces driving arms control.   On one hand is the military-industrial complex's need for an enemy to help justify its size and power, which pushes the arms race. The second aspect of this dynamic is the general public, who fear nuclear weaponry, and try to restrain its development and use (Public Lecture, Massachusetts Institute of Technology, November 1, 1986).

4.   It is somewhat ironic that the ideas of George Kennan, through his containment article in 1947 and his later renunciation of that approach, have been important in both camps.

5.   President Reagan long sought a "defensive" orientation, previously being enamored of the civil defense variants (Scheer 1982).

6.   During the Summer Seminar on Arms Control and Nuclear Weapons at MIT and Harvard in June 1986, an exchange illustrated viewpoints near the extremes of this debate.   One participant from the War Colleges insisted vehemently that, since the US did not yet have enough warheads to obliterate all forty thousand identified targets in the Soviet Union, therefore arms control was out of the question.   In response, Professor George Rathjens of Massachusetts Institute of Technology related his view of the 1950's SIOP (the existing targeting plan) which assigned an outrageous overkill of seven megatons to an Hiroshima-sized Soviet city. Rathjens maintains very low numbers of warheads are effective for deterrence. Myrdal suggests a few hundred warheads for a "finite deterrence." Even a full scale conventional war could not avoid deaths on both sides in the scores of millions, and destruction far beyond historical precedent.   After all, neither side could plausibly   anticipate   a   scenario   like   the Malvinas/Falklands dispute.   There   damage was limited to military personnel and isolated islands rather than to the combatant countries.

7.   In the end, the Reagan Administration became unsettled by its own proposals and backed away from the substance of these discussions.   While the technicians worked tirelessly just in case, Reagan lacked the political will to achieve so much if it meant compromising on Star Wars.   It appears that some members of the Reagan Administration really sought a political symbol to parade before the electorate prior to November's

Nuclear Weapons in the University Classroom

elections, rather than a genuine agreement. Why else would they have done so little preparatory work for the substance of the negotiations? Unlike the Soviet nego- tiators, the Americans brought few military advisors, and they had not consulted with NATO allies in advance.

By the end of the session, some Administration players were reportedly walking around in a daze overwhelmed by the deliberations, while others seemed relieved (Kaplan 1986; Gelb 1986; Gordon 1986).

Nonetheless, the American public seemed to sup- port scuttling the Reykjavik proposals in order to protect Reagan's Star Wars proposal, a major employment program for the aerospace and communications industries and a new porkbarrel opportunity for members of the Senate Armed Services Committee (Council on Economic Priorities 1986). Although several compromises on Star Wars were put forward by experts in the wake of Reykjavik, the Reagan Administration was not interested in pursuing them (Chayes 1986).

8. According to a CBS/New York Times poll (October 16, 1986) voters were little moved by foreign policy issues in the 1986 elections, with less than five per- cent claiming foreign policy as a main reason for vot- ing as they did. Nevertheless, the issues of arms con- trol, nuclear weapons and military spending are likely to return to the center of the political stage. Such issues are more important for presidential than Con- gressional elections. Candidates and voters will likely spend more time on these issues in future elec- tions.

REFERENCES

Blacker, Coit D. 1987. Reluctant Warriors: The United States, The Soviet Union, and Arms Control. New York: W.H. Freeman and Company.

Blacker, Coit D., and Gloria Duffey, eds. 1984. In- ternational Arms Control, 2d. Stanford, CA: Stanford University Press.

Chayes, Antonia Handler, and Abram Chayes. 1986. New York Times. October 16.

Cockburn, Andrew. 1984. The Threat: Inside the So- viet Military Machine. New York: Vintage Books.

Council on Economic Priorities. 1986. <u>Report</u>. November.

Dellums, Ronald, ed. 1983. <u>Defense Sense</u>. Cambridge, MA: Ballinger Publishing Company.

Fallows, James. 1982. <u>National Defense</u>. New York: Vintage Books.

Gaddis, John Lewis. 1982. <u>Strategies of Containment</u>. New York: Oxford University Press.

Gansler, Jacques. 1980. <u>The Defense Industry</u>. Cambridge: The MIT Press.

Gelb, Leslie. 1986. <u>New York Times</u>. October 16.

Gordon, Michael R. 1986. <u>New York Times</u>. October 16.

Gottemoeller, Rose E. 1986. "Soviet Arms Control Decision Making Since Brezhnev." In <u>The Soviet Calculus of Nuclear War</u>, edited by Roman Kolkowicz and Ellen Propper Miciewicz. Lexington, MA: Lexington Books.

Harris, John, and Eric Markusen, eds. 1986. <u>Nuclear Weapons and the Threat of Nuclear War</u>. San Diego: Harcourt Brace Jovanovich.

Harvard Nuclear Study Group. 1983. <u>Living With Nuclear Weapons</u>. New York: Bantam Books.

Jervis, Robert. 1984. <u>The Illogic of American Nuclear Strategy</u>. Ithaca: Cornell University Press.

Kaplan, Fred. 1983. <u>The Wizards of Armegaddon</u>. New York: Simon and Schuster.

Kaplan, Fred. 1986. <u>Boston Globe</u>. November 2.

Kaufmann, William W. 1986. <u>A Reasonable Defense</u>. Washington, DC: The Brookings Institution.

Kegley, Charles, and Eugene R. Wittkopf, eds. 1985. <u>The Nuclear Reader</u>. New York: St. Martin's Press.

Kennan, George F. 1979. "Needed: A New American View of the USSR." In <u>Detente or Debacle: Common Sense in U.S.-Soviet Relations</u>, edited by Fred Warner Neal. New York: W.W. Norton & Company.

Kovel, Joel. 1983. <u>Against the State of Nuclear Terror</u>. Boston: South End Press.

Lamb, Christopher J. 1988. <u>How to Think about Arms Control, Disarmament, and Defense</u>. Englewood Cliffs, NJ: Prentice Hall.

Lasswell, Harold D. 1950. <u>Politics: Who Gets What, When, How</u>. New York: Peter Smith.

Mack, John E. 1986. "The Psychological Impact of Nuclear Arms Competition in Children and Adolescents." In <u>Nuclear Weapons and the Threat of Nuclear War</u>, edited by John Harris and Eric Markusen. San Diego: Harcourt Brace Jovanovich.

Manhoff, Robert Karl. 1986. "The Media: Nuclear Secrecy vs Democracy." In <u>Nuclear Weapons and the Threat of Nuclear War</u>, edited by John Harris and Eric Markusen. San Diego: Harcourt Brace Jovanovich.

Miller, Steven, ed. 1984. <u>Strategy and Nuclear Deterrence</u>. Princeton, NJ: Princeton University Press.

Myrdal, Alva. 1982. <u>The Game of Disarmament</u>, Revised. New York: Pantheon Books.

Nacht, Michael. 1985. <u>The Age of Vulnerability: Threats to the Nuclear Stalemate</u>. Washington, DC: The Brookings Institution.

National Public Radio. "All Things Considered." November 6, 1986; March 27, 1987.

"NOVA: Nuclear War for Beginners." n.d. WGBH Public Television, Boston.

Schell, Jonathon. 1984. <u>The Abolition</u>. New York: Alfred A. Knopf.

Scribner, Richard A., Theodore J. Ralston, and William D. Metz. 1985. <u>The Verification Challenge: Problems and Promise of Strategic Nuclear Arms Control Verification</u>. Boston: Birkhäuser.

Sheer, Robert. 1982. <u>With Enough Shovels</u>. New York: Random House.

The Political Core

Talbott, Strobe. 1984. <u>Deadly Gambits</u>. New York:
Alfred A. Knopf.

<u>Teaching Political Science</u>. 14 (Spring 1987).

Wolfe, Alan, and Jerry Sanders. 1979. "Resurgent Cold
War Ideology: The Case of the Committee on the Present
Danger." In <u>Capitalism and the State in U.S.-Latin
American Relations</u>, edited by Richard Fagan. Stanford,
CA: Stanford University Press.

Yergin, Daniel. 1977. <u>The Shattered Peace</u>. Boston:
Houghton Miflin Company.

CHAPTER 3: VALUE CHOICES AND CROSS-CULTURAL AWARENESS

John MacDougall

University of Lowell

In an undergraduate course I teach on "Nuclear Weapons, Values and Society," efforts are made to increase students' awareness of value choices and cultural factors underlying policies concerning development and stockpiling of nuclear weapons. This chapter describes the course and some classroom activities used to direct students' attention to the value choices and cultural contexts of nuclear policies.

NUCLEAR WEAPONS, VALUES AND SOCIETY

This is an introductory course with no prerequisites offered since 1983 by the Sociology Department at the University of Lowell, Massachusetts, a state institution with about 10,000 full time students. (1) It is cross-listed in the interdisciplinary Technology and Human Values program, and also in the Peace and Conflict Studies program. The course usually has two sections of 100 students. It can be taken to meet the university core requirement in social science, and also to fulfill a core requirement that undergraduates take a course on human values. Most students enrolling in the course are juniors and seniors majoring in engineering or science.

Most students at the University of Lowell are in technical and professional fields. Typically, undergraduates are the first generation in their families in college, from a blue-collar or lower white-collar background. They usually commute to class (MacDougall, 1985).

The nuclear weapons course has two primary goals. The first is to give students a greater awareness of the value choices involved, and an ability to make informed choices as citizens or defense specialists and decision makers. I want both specialists and citizens to realize that they have to make choices on nuclear weapons (avoiding the issues is itself a choice) and that those choices are bound to be shaped by certain general values.

The second primary goal of the course is to teach the main social science concepts and generalizations involved in understanding nuclear weapons. This is valuable for its own sake, and because the course meets the university's social science core requirement. But social science awareness is also needed because it is essential to cultural and value awareness.

Social scientific awareness is important here for several reasons. For one, superpower conflicts and Third World conflicts liable to escalate to world war are largely shaped by very deep cultural and ideological divisions. Thus when conflicting parties attempt to communicate there is often a grave risk of their merely talking past each other. To minimize this risk in the next generation of citizens, and to help students better grasp the nature of these divisions, several major social scientific topics need to be covered in my course. They include not only cultures and ideologies, and their role in creating divisions; but also other topics such as blueprints and proposals for going beyond current cultural divisions, as discussed below.

Another important reason for students to seriously study social science aspects of the topic is so they may better understand the social dynamics influencing the behavior of individuals, of institutions, social classes and other social categories, as they choose values and create their cultures. In other words, I want students to develop as much sociological imagination as possible (see Mills, 1959).

To a lesser degree, I try to develop a historical awareness since legacies of the past are often of great sociological importance. Thus I give two lectures on Russian and Soviet history. In addition, I teach a few basic scientific and technological concepts, such as the differences between nuclear fusion and fission, and between single warhead and MIRVed missiles. On these topics I rely largely on colleagues from the university's physics and radiological science departments, who are guest speakers and serve as resource people. An important reason for this is to demystify the language of nuclear technology for non-science and non-engineering majors in the course.

Few students in the course have had more than three college-level social science courses. There is also a widespread campus culture of noninvolvement in controversial issues, stemming largely from the demographics of the university described above. Another problem is an attitude common among engineering majors and some engineering faculty that liberal arts courses should be easy and "gotten out of the way" so students can concentrate on their "real" courses. On the other hand, engineering students are often considered the elite of the university, and students in my course are generally mature, articulate and hard working.

If students expect a "gut" course, they are in for a shock. I require about 75 pages of reading each week, about a quarter of it serious social scientific analysis. I assign three types of written work. Five multiple-choice quizzes cover readings and lectures. These are designed especially to ensure students do the reading. The second major assignment is a paper comparing Soviet and American magazine articles. The third is a final paper based on students' participation in a mock world disarmament and peace conference. These two assignments are discussed below.

The class spends one or two weeks on each of the following topics: war and weapons before 1945; how nuclear weapons work and their main biological and ecological effects; the history of nuclear weapons and strategic doctrines; Soviet history and society, and their strategic and diplomatic implications; arms control efforts past and present; explanations of the superpowers' nuclear policies (including cultural, economic and historical factors); possible causes of world war in developing countries (focusing on Central America); and alternatives to nuclear deterrence which range from modest proposals to utopian visions.

Required readings are selected to provide a vivid historical view of World War I (Remarque, 1956); a general reader (Harris and Markusen, 1985); a personal view of the USSR (Walker, 1986); perspectives on developing countries (Coalition for a New Foreign Policy, 1985; Berryman, 1985), and alternative security policies (Fischer, 1984).

VALUES AND CULTURES: CLASS ASSIGNMENTS

To introduce the notion of value choices, on the first two days of class I have students do an exercise. They think for five minutes, then discuss in groups of three, about: (a) the priorities they give to security, progress and freedom; and (b) their ranking of various careers such as manager of a high-technology company, state senator, and teacher in a developing country.

Partly using these examples, I then define and discuss a value roughly as a general condition that one considers desirable and is willing to strive for. Early in the semester, I also introduce the concept of culture, discussed below.

In the middle of the semester, after students have read and heard lectures on the Soviet Union, I assign a major paper comparing Soviet and American values. For this they select on article from <u>Soviet Life</u> magazine and another from <u>Life</u> (on which <u>Soviet Life</u> is modeled). Students must pick out and compare major values expressed in each article, citing specific sentences. I explain beforehand that value judgments can be implicit, and give examples of how such judgments can be detected.

For the final major assignment, I have the class participate in a mock world disarmament and peace conference. For this they are assigned at random to a wide range of roles. These include: UN Secretary General; American and Soviet Air Force generals; American priest; Soviet teacher (assumed to be active in the Peace Committee); Soviet steel worker; Soviet central Asian farm worker; British steelworker (perhaps unemployed); Japanese journalist; Polish shipyard worker and housewife; Israeli teacher and general; Palestinian student and peasant; Nicaraguan student and businessperson; Salvadoran peasant (perhaps guerila supporter); Foreign Minister of India; Nigerian oil worker; black South African miner; and Chinese textile worker.

The list of roles is designed so that there are relatively few from the US or Western Europe. I require that students in certain roles hold pacifist values (these include a Soviet teacher, American priest, Polish shipyard worker, Japanese journalist, and Nicaraguan student).

Value Choices and Cross-Cultural Awareness

Students have to write and deliver orally a three page speech in their roles. The speech is based on a small amount of library research. It deals with what should be done about (a) nuclear weapons; and (b) either world trouble-spots (which could include the student's adopted "country"), or socioeconomic justice. Before they write their speeches, groups of students in each role have brief conferences with me, in which I give them some background about their countries and suggest readings. Students playing uneducated people are allowed to say they know nothing about nuclear weapons, but it is assumed they hold definite views on trouble-spots and socioeconomic justice.

For the presentations of students' speeches, the class divides into caucuses of 5-8 students based on their regions of origin, and focusing on either trouble-spots or socioeconomic justice, in addition to nuclear weapons. The caucuses first meet about a month before the end of the semester, as a way of getting students to start this assignment promptly. The caucuses then meet again near the end of the semester, to take account of what was said at the previous caucus session, and to write an agreed communique.

On the last two days of the semester, the whole class reconvenes. At first students continue to play their roles: they hear reports from their caucuses and seek to reach worldwide agreements. Finally, they become themselves, try again to reach agreements and debrief on the whole experience.

The final paper students write has to contain the final version of their speeches to their caucuses, with a brief annotated bibliography of items other than required readings. The final paper also contains comments on such matters as what they have learned from the conference about power in societies and their views of the relative importance of power vs. ideology in shaping American or Soviet nuclear policies.

To further stimulate value and cultural awareness, and to foster student participation in such large classes, I break the class down into discussion groups about every three weeks. The groups, consisting of about six students, are given suggested topics beforehand. These include: What would you have done if you had been on the panel hearing the Oppenheimer security case in 1953-54? What does security mean to you? Do you agree with Churchill that in the nuclear age "survival [will be] the twin brother of annihilation"? Will "Star Wars" work? What are your first memories of communism? What are the main causes of conflicts in Central America?

After Soviet history and society have been presented, I have students pair off, with one playing the role of a Soviet citizen and the other interviewing him or her. After the interviews, I ask the groups to discuss assumptions made by each party and their sources of information (2). I deliberately choose discussion topics that are provocative and I welcome students injecting their values. But I also encourage serious discussion of sociological and historical questions.

In the first discussion group, I have students share their emotional reactions to nuclear war. This discussion group is also attended by staff from the university's Counseling Center who are trained in counseling students about these emotions. At the ensuing meeting of the full class I go over their emotional reactions. I do not think it is appropriate in this course for students to analyze those emotions in depth. But I want students to consider it acceptable to talk about them, and to know that counseling help is available.

As a final source of diversity in covering value and cultural issues, I show movies and bring in guest speakers. Movies include "The Day After Trinity" (on Oppenheimer's life and times), "Atomic Cafe" (a sardonic collage of media coverage in the 1940s and 1950s), and "Video from Russia" (informal interviews by an American journalist of a diverse group of Soviet people). I refer to the first two movies in several lectures. In one discussion group session, students deal with the Oppenheimer hearings, as discussed above, and in another session they are asked what they would do if they were interviewed by a Soviet journalist.

Guest speakers have included visiting Soviet students and scientists; ROTC officers (one of whom formerly commanded an ICBM silo crew); a scientist doing classified work for a major military research and development company; and activists and journalists working for conversion of military facilities to civilian use.

VALUES AND CULTURES: THEMES AND OUTCOMES

What substantive topics are covered, and with what success? Throughout the course, I refer to two central areas on which different value judgments are made. The first of these is loyalty: to one's family, one's community, the world, future generations, and so on. I point out that loyalties can vary in intensity. The second area is rationality, defined as a systematic and dispassionate linking of means and ends. Other value-related words that keep cropping up include security and progress.

By the end of the semester, all students acquire some sense of the importance of choosing between different loyalties when one considers nuclear-weapons issues. Most students appear to gain at least some awareness that alternative nuclear policies should be judged in the light of some standard of rationality. Probably many students perceive that different groups in America have different standards of rationality when it comes to national security.

Students came to see that, in general, humans must choose between major values. They also gained a vivid sense that there exist widely divergent values in the world, a divergence largely explicable by societal differences in cultural assumptions, class structures, historical experiences, and so on. Students realize that for millions of poor people on this planet, social justice and local tranquility are more important than nuclear arms control. The final paper and, to a lesser extent, the assignment on Soviet and American magazines are very helpful in raising awareness of these points.

In the Soviet-American magazine assignment, students do quite well at spotting explicit values. But they do not do so well at detecting implicit ones or distinguishing concrete norms from abstract values. This requires some care and sensitivity in instructions for the assignment, and affords opportunities for thought-provoking comments from the faculty member evaluating students' written work.

Another problem concerns the students' lack of sophistication in choosing specific alternative values and in relating values to each other. Thus they often do not have a very good understanding of loyalties to different territorial units: for example, they may not

53

easily grasp that a Nicaraguan student might choose loyalty to his or her country over loyalty to his or her family or social class.

Further, students often do not easily see that there can be conflicts between values. Thus, regarding security and progress, few realize that weapons embodying the latest technological progress might pose an increased danger to a nation's or the world's security. These problems seem particularly serious with regard to radical alternatives to nuclear deterrence. For instance, many seem unable to grasp that conversion of military facilities to civilian use might increase a country's economic strength and democratic participation, even though it might harm military security in a "hardware" sense.

Usually, students do not easily comprehend that values can shift, or the processes whereby such shifts occur. Thus, most students assume that Soviet leaders have since 1917 always assigned top priority to controlling the population. Few recognize that economic progress and political liberalization since Stalin's death might have affected the public's values.

Virtually all these students prefer talking about the world's problems to shooting one's way to a solution. In the mock world conference most students develop a vivid sense of the basic interests they have at stake in the roles they play. Perhaps it is impossible, given the depth of conflicts between Soviet and American generals, or Israeli generals and Palestinian students, to go beyond the bland generalities that caucuses and conference usually produce. But hardly anyone has even begun to relate broad values to specific interests, in the form of concrete peace or disarmament proposals. Thus, students playing Soviet and American generals rarely consider the possibility that they might share a value of common security, or look at how this value might be realized through collaborative civilian projects or cooperative measures to prevent nuclear proliferation.

Still, some students have made insightful comments on these matters, as is evident in the following quotations from some final papers. A psychology major (enrolled in a special program at the university for former housewives returning to college) said in her role as a Salvadoran peasant: "Now that I have taken an active role in this war, I see how much so many of the women have done for our cause. Many women have come from the cities to fight with the guerillas. They tell me that many housewives and women teachers are getting together to fight for help for the children, child care, jobs and safe birth control. This is what I want for my country."

An electrical engineering major playing the part of the UN Secretary General remarked: ."In Bangladesh, a group of 20 poor women were given a loan of $170 by the International Fund for Agricultural Development. They used this money to buy cows and start a small dairy business. They are now well on their way to being self-sufficient and enjoying modest economic well -being. I assume many among us today have recently spent $170 on something as frivolous as a restaurant bill or a new suit of clothing. It is sobering to see how much can be done, by so little, for someone in a struggling Third World community." A computer science major in the role of a British steel worker said: "We have spent billions of pounds on [anti-terrorist] campaigns only to have Irish Republican Army terrorism brought to England. These billions could be more productively spent in revitalizing the British steel industry. I am not speaking to save my job, but for the good of the entire country."

Final papers often contained many thoughtful and detailed recommendations, both when students played their roles and when they spoke for themselves. Unfortunately, space does not permit discussion of specific recommendations.

What about efforts to teach basic sociological concepts and generalizations? As so often happens with technically-oriented people, students showed much greater interest in, and mastery over, concrete details than abstract ideas. Still, many students demonstrated in their speeches to the world conference that they had learned much about countries on which they knew virtually nothing at the beginning of the semester.

In this course, three central sociological concepts are constantly reiterated, and often featured in quizzes. One is power, or the ability of a social group or individual to gain what is in its interests, despite opposition. The other pair of concepts are culture and ideology. Culture is defined as a set of values and assumptions shared by a group of people of any size. Ideology is taken to mean a shared package of diagnoses, prescriptions and prognoses oriented to solving major problems in society. In my lectures I repeatedly distinguish between conservative, liberal and radical (or pacifist) ideologies, and their associated values. I often discussed the usefulness of these ideologies in forming nuclear-weapons policies.

In my experience, all students in the course have recognized that power is very often a factor in the nuclear arms race. Students also become aware of the great diversity of human cultures. They gain a general understanding of conservatism, liberalism and pacifism. Through material on the USSR, they became reasonably knowledgeable--and respectful--about Russian culture. They seem to develop a good intuitive sense that all social groups' and individuals' values are deeply influenced by their cultures.

However, that was about as far as most students went. For instance, not many could see that advocacy of a multilayered "Star Wars" defense required great faith in the ideology of technological fixes. In their final papers, not many students made the connection between (a) power relations between the nuclear nations and (b) the dynamics of world hunger or conventional war. Nor did students show much appreciation of the subtler interrelations between forms of power, for example between coercion and ideological hegemony. There was little awareness of how the Kremlin's foreign and military policies might be shaped by domestic forces, such as concern over Moslem fundamentalism in Soviet Central Asia. Few seemed to have a good grasp of the dynamics of ideology; thus they had trouble responding to the charge that all Soviet publications are propaganda.

Still, some interesting comments were made on power and ideology in the best student papers. In one final paper, a mathematics major (speaking for herself) remarked: "Power seems to lead to more power. Once a person has power over someone else, rather than giving it up, they seem to look for a wider sphere of influence." An English major reported: "In addition to the idea that power and wealth are closely related, the majority of our caucus also believed that power is self-perpetuating. This theory is evident in the United

States in the symbiotic relationship between the government and industry. In countries like El Salvador and Nicaragua, this theory is evident in the manner in which the old landowners used their land to increase their [monetary] wealth, which in turn was used to purchase yet more land."

On connections between poverty or trouble spots and nuclear weapons, a "Soviet general" (in real life a political science major and ROTC cadet) said: "[In the Persian Gulf] the ongoing war threatens an explosion in a potentially volatile area. The USSR and US share the common interest of balancing power in that region, thus limiting the possibility of the confrontation expanding." A "student from Nicaragua" (the aforementioned English major) commented: "I have seen the improvements brought about by the Sandinistas. I believe the only threat posed by the Sandinistas is the threat that the United States is creating for itself in its attempts to destabilize the Nicaraguan government. Perhaps the reaction of the US towards having a Soviet-backed government in Nicaragua can be traced to the Cuban missile crisis."

On culture, an undeclared liberal arts major (atypically, a freshman) who played the part of a Palestinian student, remarked, speaking for himself: "When we argued [in our caucus] about the West Bank, through the use of cultural identity I found that each faction was able to reaffirm [its] right to use of the land. Culture gives people something to identify with. This sets up a kind of 'us against them.'" On ideology, the ROTC student cited earlier, stepping out of his role, commented: "Russia has been subject to autocratic and/or totalitarian rule. It is not by choice but by circumstance that ideology has grown this way in Russia. If more people understood this (and this works both ways) there would be far less tension between us."

These comments indicate a level of thoughtfulness, value and cultural awareness that suggests students have struggled successfully with basic sociological concepts and generalizations in the course. That students can, with varying degrees of success, relate these factors to policies concerning development and stockpiling of nuclear weapons in the US and USSR seems a modest contribution to nuclear education.

Nuclear Weapons in the University Classroom

NOTES

1.   Initial preparation of this course was aided by a fellowship from the World Policies Institute. Undergraduate courses at the university are numbered from the 100s to the 400s, with this one in the 200-level.

2.   I am grateful to Educators for Social Responsibility for suggesting this exercise.

REFERENCES

Berryman, Philip. 1985. Inside Central America (New York: Pantheon).

Coalition for a New Foreign Policy. 1985. "A Few Billions for Defense" (pamphlet).

Fischer, Dietrich. 1984. Preventing War in the Nuclear Age (Totowa, NJ: Rowman & Allanheld).

Harris, John B. and Markusen, Eric, eds. 1986. Nuclear Weapons and the Threat of Nuclear War (New York: Harcourt Brace).

MacDougall, John, 1985. "Teaching about Nuclear Weapons: Value Awareness and Social Scientific Analysis." Proceedings of the American Society for Engineering Education.

Mills, C. Wright. 1959. The Sociological Imagination (New York: Oxford University Press).

Remarque, Eric M. 1956. All Quiet on the Western Front (New York: Fawcett).

Walker, Martin. 1986. The Walking Giant: Gorbachev's Russia (New York: Pantheon).

CHAPTER 4: A SELECTED BIBLIOGRAPHY OF REQUIRED READINGS AND FILMS

Michael S. Hamilton

University of Southern Maine

The references in this bibliography were compiled during a survey of topics and teaching methods used recently in 75 University courses dealing with nuclear weapons technology. Over 800 references to books, monographs, articles, foundation reports and government documents are grouped here by subject headings which are generally comparable to topics identified in Chapter 1, except where there were too few items to warrant a separate heading. A brief paragraph describing the topics included will be found at the beginning of each subject grouping.

These subject groupings, while of necessity somewhat arbitrary, do not seem capricious. They are not, of course, mutually exclusive. Some titles could easily have been listed under several subject headings. Generally such titles have been listed under the subject for which they were assigned in the syllabus from which they were obtained.

The bibliography contains materials which have been selected for classroom use in recent years by one or more university faculty in the United States. These references represent required readings only, optional or supplemental readings having been omitted.

Thus, although it is lengthy, the primary value of the bibliography lies in its selectiveness. No attempt has been made to compile a comprehensive list of the scholarly works concerning nuclear weapons technology. Because books published in 1988-1989 are too new to have been widely adopted for classroom use, the bibliography does not include some significant recent texts, such as: McGeorge Bundy, Danger and Survival, (New York: Random House, 1988); or John Newhouse, War and Peace in the Nuclear Age, (New York: Knopf, 1989). However, the coverage is broad and many of the most useful teaching materials have been included. The bibliography should be useful in "self-education" efforts of faculty teaching courses on nuclear arms.

Opposing viewpoints on many issues are included in this bibliography, along with older references of historical interest. Page numbers for selected readings which have been found useful for course reading assignments are included for some longer works. A list of films used in the courses examined is included at the end of the bibliography.

Only those required readings for which reasonably complete publication information could be obtained through reference to generally available library catalogs and indexes have been reproduced here. Within each subject grouping, entries are arranged alphabetically by author, or by title where no author is given. To the extent possible, citations follow the suggestions in Kate Turabian, **A Manual for Writers of Term Papers, Theses and Dissertations**, 5th ed, (Chicago: University of Chicago Press, 1987). Items which were used in more than one course are denoted with the number of syllabi in which they appeared in parentheses following the citation, as: (4).

MOST FREQUENTLY REQUIRED READINGS

Little agreement between faculty on choice of required readings was evident, as only thirteen of over 800 references appeared in five or more of the 75 syllabi examined. Half of these were general texts, including one by Jonathan Schell which was most frequently used (in 14 courses). These are listed in alphabetical order:

Ground Zero, Inc. [Molander, Roger] **Nuclear War: What's In It For You**. New York: Ground Zero/Pocket Books, 1983. (6)

Harvard Nuclear Study Group. **Living With Nuclear Weapons**. New York: Bantam Books, 1983. (12)

Kegley, Charles W., and Eugene R. Wittkoph, eds. **The Nuclear Reader: Strategy, Weapons, War**. New York: St. Martin's, 1985. (5)

Mandelbaum, Michael. **The Nuclear Question: The United States and Nuclear Weapons 1946-1976**. New York: Cambridge University Press, 1979. (8)

Bibliography

Schell, Jonathan. The Fate of the Earth. New York:
Knopf, 1982. (14)

Sivard, Ruth. World Military and Social Expenditures,
1983. Leesburg, VA: World Priorities, 1983 (annual).
(6)

Other texts which appeared in more than five of the
syllabi examined, listed under the subject grouping
with which they were most often assigned, include:

Strategic Doctrine:

Forsberg, Randall.   "A Bilateral Nuclear Weapons
Freeze."   Scientific American 247 (November 1982):
52-61. (5)

Arms Control:

Blacker, Coit, and Gloria Duffy, eds.   International
Arms Control: Issues and Agreements, 2d ed. Palo Alto, CA: Stanford University Press, 1984. (5)

European Security:

Bundy, McGeorge, George F. Kennan, Robert S. McNamara,
and Gerard Smith. "Nuclear Weapons and the Atlantic
Alliance." Foreign Affairs 60 (1982): 753-68. (5)

History of Nuclear Weapons Development:

Hersey, John. Hiroshima. New York: Bantam Books,
1959. (8)

Effects of Nuclear Weapons:

Glasstone, S., and A. Dolan. Effects of Nuclear Weapons. 3d ed. Washington, DC: Government Printing Office, 1977. (5)

Lewis, Kevin. "The Prompt and Delayed Effects of Nuclear War." Scientific American, 241 (July 1979):
35-47.(5)

Nuclear Ethics:

US Catholic Bishops. "The Challenge of Peace: God's
Promise and Our Response". Origins, May 19, 1983. (11)

Also in: <u>The Nuclear Reader: Strategy, Weapons, War</u>, pp. 43-57. Edited by Charles W. Kegley, Jr., and Eugene R. Wittkopf. New York: St. Martin's, 1985.

By highlighting the above texts we do not mean to suggest they are the most appropriate for all teaching purposes, styles or courses, or that the subjects with which they are associated are all that should be included in a course on nuclear technology. Those are decisions for persons designing a particular course. A large number of other subjects and required readings are presented below for further consideration.

Films which were used in five or more courses examined were:

"The Day After Trinity: J. Robert Oppenheimer and the Atomic Bomb." (1981). Pyramid Film and Video, Box 1048, Santa Monica, CA 90406. 800-421-2304. (10)

"Dr. Strangelove, Or How I Learned to Stop Worrying and to Love the Bomb." (1964). RCA/Columbia Pictures Home Video, 2901 W. Alameda Ave., Burbank, CA 91505. 818-954-4590. (6)

"Hiroshima/Nagasaki, 1945." University of Arizona Film Scheduling, Bureau of Audio-Visual Services, University of Arizona, Tucson, AZ. 626-884-3872. (5)

"The War Game." International Historic Films, P.O. Box 29035, Chicago, IL. 312-436-8051. (6)

<u>GENERAL TEXTS</u>:

This section includes basic required texts for one or more courses examined plus those in which readings were assigned for two or more of the topics represented by the subject groupings in the remainder of this bibliography.

Barash, D. <u>The Arms Race and Nuclear War</u>. Belmont, CA: Wadsworth, 1987. (4)

Barton, John H. and Lawrence D. Weiler, eds. <u>International Arms Control: Issues and Agreements.</u> Palo Alto, CA: Stanford University Press, 1976. (3)

Bernstein, Barton J. <u>The Atomic Bomb: Critical Issues</u>. Boston: Little and Brown, 1976. (2)

Bibliography

Brodie, Bernard. <u>The Absolute Weapon.</u> Salem, NH: Ayer Company, 1946. (4)

Bundy, William P., ed. <u>The Nuclear Controversy: A Foreign Affairs Reader</u>. New York: New American Library, 1984. (2)

Calder, Nigel. <u>Nuclear Nightmares</u>. New York: Penguin, 1981. (3)

Carnesale, Albert, Joseph S. Nye, and Graham T. Allison. <u>Hawks, Doves, and Owls</u>. New York: W.W. Norton, 1985. (4)

Cohen, Avner, and Stephen Lee, eds. <u>Nuclear Weapons and the Future of Humanity: The Fundamental Questions</u>. Totowa, NJ: Rowman and Littlefield, 1986. (2)

Dyson, Freeman. <u>Weapons and Hope</u>. New York: Harper & Row, 1984. (3)

Fallows, James. <u>National Defense</u>. New York: Random House, 1981. (3)

Farley, Philip J., et al. <u>Arms Across the Sea</u>. Washington, DC: Brookings, 1978.

Fisher, Douglas. <u>Peacemaking</u>. Mahwah, NJ: Paulist Press, n.d.

Gaddis, John L. <u>Strategies of Containment: A Critical Appraisal of Postwar American National Security Policy</u>. New York: Oxford University Press, 1982. (3)

Gray, Colin S. <u>The Geopolitics of the Nuclear Era: Heartland, Rimlands, and the Technological Revolution</u>. New York: Crane Russak, 1977.

Gregory, D. <u>The Nuclear Predicament</u>. New York: St. Martin's, 1986. (2)

Ground Zero, Inc. [Molander, Roger] <u>Nuclear War: What's In It For You</u>. New York: Ground Zero/Pocket Books, 1983. (6)

Ground Zero, Inc. <u>What About the Russians--and Nuclear War?</u> New York: Ground Zero/Pocket Books, 1983.

Harvard Nuclear Study Group. _Living With Nuclear Weapons_. New York: Bantam Books, 1983. (8)

Herken, Greg. _Counsels of War_. New York: Knopf, 1985. (2)

Herken, Greg. _The Winning Weapon: The Atomic Bomb in the Cold War, 1945-1950_. New York: Knopf, 1981. (4)

Jervis, Robert. _Perception and Misperception in International Politics_. Princeton, NJ: Princeton University Press, 1976. (4)

Johansen, Robert C. _Toward a Dependable Peace: Proposal for an Appropriate Security System._ New York: World Policy Institute, 1978. (4)

Kahan, Jerome. _Security in the Nuclear Age_. Washington, DC: Brookings, 1975.

Kaufmann, William W. _Defense in the 1980's_. Washington, DC: Brookings, 1981.

Kegley, Charles W., and Eugene R. Wittkoph, eds. _The Nuclear Reader: Strategy, Weapons, War_. New York: St. Martin's, 1985. (5)

Kennan, George F. _The Nuclear Delusion: Soviet-American Relations in the Atomic Age_. New York: Pantheon, 1983. (3)

Kennedy, Edward F., and Mark O. Hatfield, _Freeze! How You Can Help Prevent Nuclear War_. New York: Bantam Books, 1982.(2)

Kissinger, Henry A. _Nuclear Weapons and Foreign Policy_, abr. ed. Edited by Philip Quigg. New York: Norton, 1969. (2)

Lifton, Robert J. _The Broken Connection: Death and the Continuity of Life_. New York: Simon and Schuster, 1979. (2)

Mandelbaum, Michael. _The Nuclear Future_. Ithaca, NY: Cornell University Press, 1983.

Mandelbaum, Michael. _The Nuclear Question: The United States and Nuclear Weapons 1946-1976_. New York: Cambridge University Press, 1979. (8)

Bibliography

Mandelbaum, Michael. _The Nuclear Revolution: International Politics Before and After Hiroshima_. New York: Cambridge University Press, 1981. (2)

Masuji, Ibusi. _Black Rain_. Tokyo: Kadansha International, Ltd., 1981.

Mische, Gerald, and Patricia Mische. _Toward a Human World Order: Beyond the National Security Straitjacket_. Mahwah, NJ: Paulist Press, 1977.

Patterson, Walter C. _Nuclear Power_. New York: Penguin Books, 1983.

Perry, William. _The Role of Technology in Meeting the Defense Challenges of the 1980's_. Palo Alto, CA: Stanford University Press, 1981.

Ramsey, Paul. _The Limits of Nuclear War: Thinking About the Do-Able and the Un-Do-Able_. New York: Council on International Affairs, n.d.

Reichart, John, and Steven Sturm, eds. _American Defense Policy_. 5th ed. Baltimore: Johns Hopkins University, 1982. (2)

Russett, Bruce, and Bruce Blair. _Progress in Arms Control? A Scientific American Reader_. San Francisco: W.H. Freeman, 1979. (4)

Schell, Jonathan. _The Fate of the Earth_. New York: Knopf, 1982. (14)

Schelling, Thomas C. _Arms and Influence_. New Haven: Yale, 1966. (4)

Schroeer, Dietrich, _Science, Technology, and the Nuclear Arms Race_. New York: John Wiley, 1984. (4)

Scientific American. _Arms Control and the Arms Race: Readings from Scientific American_. New York: W.H. Freeman, 1973. (5)

Sivard, Ruth. _World Military and Social Expenditures, 1983_. Leesburg, VA: World Priorities, 1983 (annual). (5)

Smoke, Richard. _National Security and the Nuclear Dilemma_. Reading, MA: Addison-Wesley, 1984. (4)

Nuclear Weapons in the University Classroom

Spanier, John. *Games Nations Play*, 5th ed. Washington, DC: Congressional Quarterly, 1984.

Stephenson, C.M., ed. *Alternative Methods for International Security*. Washington, DC: University Press, 1982.

Stephenson, C.M., K.E. Boulding, and W.A. Reardon, eds. *Problems of War and Peace: A Book of Readings*. Hamilton, NY: Colgate University, 1983.

Talbott, Strobe. *Deadly Gambits*. New York: Vintage, 1985.

Talbott, Strobe. *Endgame: The Inside Story of SALT II*. New York: Harper & Row, 1980. (3)

Tsipis, Kosta. *Arsenal: Understanding Weapons in the Nuclear Age*. New York: Simon and Schuster, 1984. (3)

Union of Concerned Scientists. *Briefing Manual: A Collection of Materials on Nuclear Weapons and Arms Control*. Cambridge, MA: Union of Concerned Scientists, 1983.

Union of Concerned Scientists. *Toward a New Security: Lessons of the Forty Years Since Trinity*. Cambridge, MA: Union of Concerned Scientists, 1985.

Wieseltier, Leon. *Nuclear War, Nuclear Peace*. New York: Holt and Co., 1983.

Williams, Robert C., and Philip L. Cantelon. *The American Atom*. Philadelphia: University of Pennsylvania Press, 1984. (2)

Yergin, Daniel. *Shattered Peace: The Origins of the Cold War and the National Security State*. Boston: Houghton Mifflin, 1977.

INTERNATIONAL RELATIONS THEORY:

This section includes discussions of theories of international political, economic and social change; dependence and interdependence; conflict, aggression, cooperation, balance of power, national power (and its elements), coercion, war, alliances, foreign and national security policy making, national interest, cultural and economic imperialism, and containment.

66

Bibliography

Arendt, Hannah. <u>On Violence</u>. San Diego: Harcourt, Brace Jovanovich, 1970.

Art, Robert. "To What Ends Military Power." <u>International Security</u> 5 (Spring 1980): 14-35.

Art, Robert, and Robert Jervis, eds. <u>International Politics: Anarchy, Force, Political Economy, and Decision Making</u>, 2d ed. Boston: Little and Brown, 1984.

Art, Robert, and Kenneth Waltz. <u>The Use of Force: International Politics and Foreign Policy</u>. Boston: Little and Brown, 1971. (2)

Barnet, Richard J. <u>Roots of War</u>. Baltimore: Penguin Books, 1972. (3)

Beyond War Foundation. <u>Beyond War: A New Way of Thinking</u>. Palo Alto: Beyond War Foundation, 1985.

Blechman, Barry, and Douglas Hart. "The Political Utility of Nuclear Weapons: The 1973 Middle East Crisis." <u>International Security</u> 7 (Summer 1982): 132-56. (2)

Brodie, Bernard. <u>War and Politics</u>. New York: MacMillan, 1973. (2)

Brown, Peter G. "...In the National Interest." In: <u>Human Rights and US Foreign Policy: Principles and Applications</u>. Edited by Peter G. Brown. Lexington, MA: Lexington Books, 1979.

Buzan, Barry. <u>People, States, and Fear: A Conceptual Introduction to the Role of Force in International Relations</u>. Chapel Hill, NC: University of North Carolina Press, 1983.

Chamberlain, Neville. "In Defense of Munich." In: <u>The Struggle for Peace</u>. London: Hutchinson, 1940.

Chomsky, Noam. <u>Human Rights and American Foreign Policy</u>. Nottingham, England: Spokesman Books, 1978.

Chomsky, Noam. "The United States versus Human Rights in the Third World." <u>Monthly Review</u>, July-August 1977, pp. 22-45.

Dougherthy, James E., and Robert L. Pfaltzgraff, <u>Con</u>-<u>tending Theories in International Relations: A Com</u>-<u>prehensive Survey</u>. New York: Harper & Row, 1980.

Durant, Will, and Ariel Durant. <u>The Lessons of His</u>-<u>tory</u>. New York: Simon and Schuster, 1960. Ch. 8, 9.

Fisher, Roger. <u>International Conflict for Beginners</u>. Magnolia, MA: Peter Smith Publishers, n.d.

Frost, J.V. "Henry Steele Commager on US Foreign Poli-cy in the '80's." <u>Worldview</u> 24 (July, 1981): 5-7.

Galtung, Johan. "The Real World." In: <u>How the World Works</u>. Edited by Gary L. Olson. Glenview, IL: Scott Foresman, 1984.

Graebner, Norman A. <u>The National Security</u>. Oxford: Oxford University Press, 1986.

Grindal, Bruce. "The Peril of Progress and the Need for Synergetic Consciousness." <u>Anthropology and Hu</u>-<u>manism Quarterly</u> 7 (March 1982): 2-10.

Halperin, Morton H. <u>Nuclear Fallacy</u>. Cambridge: Bal-linger, 1987.

Herz, John H. "Idealist Internationalism and the Secu-rity Dilemma." <u>World Politics</u> 2 (January 1950): 157-80.

Hoffman, Stanley. <u>Security in an Age of Turbulence</u>. Adelphi Paper 167. London: International Institute for Strategic Studies. 1981.

Huntington, Samuel. <u>The Soldier and the State: The Theory and Politics of Civil-Military Relations</u>. Cam-bridge, MA: Harvard University Press, 1981.

Jaquette, Jane S. "Women and Modernization Theory." <u>World Politics</u> 34 (January 1982): 267-85.

Jervis, Robert. "The Nuclear Revolution and the Common Defense." <u>Political Science Quarterly</u> 101 (1986): 689-703.

Kagan, Donald. "Human Rights, Moralism, and Foreign Policy." <u>Washington Quarterly</u> 6 (Winter 1983).

Bibliography

Karis, Thomas G. "South African Liberation: The Communist Factor." Foreign Affairs 65 (Winter 1986-87): 267-87.

Karp, Walter. The Politics of War. New York: Harper & Row, 1979.

Katzenbach, Edward L., and Gene Z. Hanrahan, "The Revolutionary Strategy of Mao Tse Tung." Political Science Quarterly 70 (1955): 321-40.

Keohane, Robert O., and Joseph S. Nye. Power and Interdependence: World Politics in Transition. Boston: Little, Brown, 1977.

Kim, Samuel S. The Quest for a Just World Order. Boulder, CO: Westview Press, 1984.

Klare, Michael T. War Without End. New York: Knopf, 1972.

Landau, Saul. "Understanding Revolution: A Guide for Critics." Monthly Review 39 (May 1987): 1-13.

Leffler, Melvyn. "The American Conception of National Security and the Beginnings of the Cold War, 1945-48." American Historical Review, (April 1982): 346-81.

McNeil, William. The Pursuit of Power: Technology, Armed Force, and Society since A.D. 1000. Chicago: University of Chicago Press, 1984.

Mellanby, Jean. "The Death of the Soul in Cuba and Communist China." International Journal on World Peace 4 (January/March 1987): 23-32/

Moore, Barrington, Jr. Reflections on the Causes of Human Misery. Boston: Beacon Press, 1972.

Oglesby, Carl. Containment and Change. New York: MacMillan, 1967.

Organski, A.K.F. World Politics. 2d ed. New York: Knopf, 1968.

Ramsey, Paul. The Just War. New York: Scribner's, 1968.

Ray, James Lee. <u>Global Politics</u>. Boston: Houghton Mifflin, 1987.

Shoup, L., and W. Minter. <u>Imperial Brain Trust: The Council on Foreign Relations and US Foreign Policy</u>. New York: Monthly Review Press, 1977.

Smoke, Richard. "National Security Affairs." In: <u>Handbook of Political Science</u>, vol. 8, <u>International Politics</u>, pp. 247-362. Edited by Nelson W. Polsby and Fred I. Greenstein. Reading, MA: Addison-Wesley, 1975.

Sommer, Mark. <u>Beyond the Bomb, Living Without Nuclear Weapons: A Field Guide to Alternative Strategies for Building a Stable Peace</u>. Chestnut Hill, MA: Expro Press, 1986.

Stoessinger, John. <u>Why Nations Go to War</u>, 3d ed. New York: St. Martin's Press, 1982.

Thompson, E.P. <u>The Heavy Dancers: Writings on War, Past and Future</u>. New York: Pantheon, 1985.

Thucydides. <u>The Peloponesian War</u>. Edited by Terry Wick. New York: Random House, 1982. (2)

Von Clauswitz, Carl. <u>On War</u>. Mattituck, NY: Amereon, n.d. (4)

Von Clauswitz, Carl. <u>War, Politics, and Power</u>. Washington, DC: Reghery Books, 1962.

Wagner, Harrison. "The Theory of Games and the Problem of International Cooperation." <u>American Political Science Review</u> 77 (1983): 330-46.

Walsh, Roger. <u>Staying Alive: The Psychology of Human Survival</u>. Boulder, CO: Shambhala Publications, 1984. (2)

Walzer, Michael. <u>Just and Unjust Wars.</u> New York: Basic Books, 1977. (4)

Waterlow, Charlotte, <u>Superpowers and Victims: The Outlook for World Community</u>. Englewood Cliffs, NJ: Prentice-Hall, 1974.

Bibliography

NATURE OF THE THREAT:

This section includes discussions of US and Soviet perceptions, motivations, and attitudes toward each other based on historical, cultural, ideological, economic and other social factors, with treatment of the "cold war" and detente.

Abrams, Nancy E., and Joel E. Primack. "The Public and Technological Decisions." Bulletin of Atomic Scientists 36 (June 1980): 44-48.

Adler, Les K., and Thomas G. Paterson. "Red Fascism: The Merger of Nazi Germany and Soviet Russia in the American Image of Totalitarianism, 1930's-1950's." American Historical Review 75 (1970).

Barnaby, Frank. "Military Scientists." Bulletin of Atomic Scientists 37 (June/July 1981): 11-12.

Beres, Louis Rene. "Steps Toward a New Planetary Identity." Bulletin of Atomic Scientists 37 (February 1981): 43-47.

Bronfenbrenner, Urie. "The Mirror Image in Soviet-American Relations: A Social Psychologist's Report." Journal of Social Issues 17 (1961): 3.

Brown, Lester R., et al. The State of the World, 1988. New York: W.W. Norton, 1988. (annual)

Casper, Barry M., and Lawrence M. Krauss. "Fortune Favors the Prepared Mind: A Movement Against Nuclear War." Science, Technology and Human Values 7 (Fall 1981): 20-26.

Center for Defense Information. "Soviet Geopolitical Momentum: Myth or Menace?" Defense Monitor 9 (1980). (2)

Chalk, Rosemary. "The Miners' Canary." Bulletin of Atomic Scientists 38 (Feb. 1982): 16-22.

Cheever, John. The Wapshot Scandal. New York: Ballantine, 1983.

Cohen, Stephen. "Sovieticus." The Nation, April 9, 1983, p. 419.

Nuclear Weapons in the University Classroom

Cracraft, James, ed. <u>The Soviet Union Today: An In-
terpretive Guide</u>. Chicago: University of Chicago
Press, 1983.

Dallin, Alexander. "The United States in the Soviet
Perspective." In: <u>Prospects of Soviet Power in the
1980's</u>, pp. 31-39. Edited by Christoph Bertram. Ham-
den, CT: Shoestring Press, 1980.

Day, Samuel H., Jr. "Captain Coleman's Challenging Job
and Why He Decided to Leave It." <u>Progressive</u>, August
1981, pp 27-31.

Day, Samuel H., Jr. "Reinventing the World." <u>Pro-
gressive</u>, March, 1982, pp. 13-14.

Doty, Paul, et al. "Nuclear War by 1999?." <u>Currents</u>,
January 1976, pp. 32-47.

Douglass, Joseph, and Almoretta Hoeber. <u>Soviet Strat-
egy for Nuclear War</u>. Palo Alto, CA: Hoover Institu-
tion Press, 1979.

Ermath, Fritz. "Contrasts in Soviet and American Stra-
tegic Thought." <u>International Security</u> 3 (Fall 1978).

Evangelista, Matthew. "The New Soviet Approach to Se-
curity." <u>World Policy Journal</u> 3 (Fall 1986): 561-99.

Falk, Richard, et al. "How A Nuclear War Could Start."
<u>Bulletin of Atomic Scientists</u> 35 (April 1979): 22-27.

Feld, Bernard T. "The Clock Stands Still." <u>Bulletin of
Atomic Scientists</u> 38 (January 1982): 1.

Feld, Bernard T. "The Hands Move Closer to Midnight."
<u>Bulletin of Atomic Scientists</u> 37 (January 1981: 1.

Harries, Owen. "Best Case Thinking." <u>Commentary</u>, May
1984, pp. 23-28.

Holloway, David. <u>The Soviet Union and the Arms Race</u>,
2d ed. New Haven: Yale University Press, 1984. (4)

Holloway, David. "War, Militarism, and the Soviet
State." <u>Alternatives</u> 6 (1980): 59-92. Also in: <u>Pro-
test and Survive</u>, pp. 70-107. Edited by E.P. Thompson
and Dan Smith. New York: Monthly Review Press, 1981.
(2)

Bibliography

Hyland, William G. "The USSR and Nuclear War." In: Rethinking the US Strategic Posture, pp. 41-76. Edited by Barry M. Blechman. New York: Ballinger, 1982.

Jamgotch, Nish, Jr. Soviet Security in Flux. Muscatine, IA: Institute Stanley Foundation, 1983.

Kaiser, R.G. Russia, The People and the Power. New York: Antheum, 1976.

Kanter, Herschel. "The Reagan Defense Program: Can It Hold Up?" Strategic Review 10 (Spring 1982): 19-34.

Kennan, George F. Memoirs, 1925-1950. Boston: Little, Brown, 1967. pp. 85-104.

Kennan, George F. "The Sources of Soviet Conduct." In: American Diplomacy, 1900-1950, pp. 107-28. Chicago: University of Chicago Press, 1951.

Kennan, George F. "Remarks." Congressional Record (House), March 17, 1988.

Lambeth, Benjamin. "How to Think About Soviet Military Doctrine." In: Soviet Strategy, pp. 105-123. Edited by John Baylis and Gerald Segal. Montclair, NJ: Allanheld & Osman, 1981.(2)

Lens, Sidney. "'You Can't Trust the Russians': The Most Dangerous Cliche." The Nation, September 11, 1982, pp. 210-211.

MccGwire, Michael. "Soviet Military Objectives." World Policy Journal 3 (Fall 1986): 667-95.

Markusen, Eric, Jeffrey Dunham, and Ronald Bee. "A Nuclear Education Campaign." Bulletin of Atomic Scientists 37 (May 1981): 39-42.

Medvedev, Roy, and Zhores Medvedev. "Nuclear Samizdat." The Nation, January 16, 1982, pp. 38-44.

Meyer, Stephen. Soviet Defense Decisionmaking. Los Angeles: Center for International and Strategic Affairs, 1982.

Nitze, Paul. "Living with the Soviets." Foreign Affairs 63 (Winter 1984/85): 360-74.

Nogee, Joseph, and Robert Donaldson. _Soviet Foreign Policy Since World War II_. Elmsford, NJ: Pergamon Press, 1981.

Pipes, Richard, "Can the Soviet Union Reform?" _Foreign Affairs_ 63 (Fall 1984): 47-61.

Pipes, Richard. "Soviet Global Strategy." _Commentary_, April 1980, pp. 31-39. (2)

Pipes, Richard. _Survival is not Enough: Soviet Realities and America's Future_. New York: Simon and Schuster, 1984.

Pipes, Richard. "Why the Soviet Union Thinks It Can Fight and Win a Nuclear War." _Commentary_, July 1977, pp. 21-34. (3)

Powers, Thomas M. "What is it About?" _Atlantic_, January, 1984, pp. 35-55.

Ross, Dennis. "Rethinking Soviet Strategic Policy: Inputs and Implications." _Journal of Strategic Studies_ 1 (May 1978): 3-30.

Sakharov, Andrei. "The Danger of Thermonuclear War: An Open Letter to Dr. Sidney Drell." _Foreign Affairs_ 61 (1983): 1001-10016.

Schell, Jonathan. "The Abolition." _New Yorker_, January 2, 1984, p.36 (part I), and January 9, 1984, p.43 (part II). (2)

Sherwin, Martin. "The Atomic Bomb and the Origins of the Cold War." _American Historical Review_ 78 (October, 1973): 945-68.

Shulman, Marshall D. "What the Russians Really Want: A Rational Response to the Soviet Challenge." _Harper's_, April, 1984, pp. 63-71.

Sivachev, Nicolai V. and Nicolai N. Yakolev. _Russia and the United States_. Chicago: University of Chicago Press, 1979. pp. 137-60.

Smith, Steve. "The Myth of the Soviet Threat." _Journal of the Royal United Services Institute_ 127 (1982): 41-49.

Bibliography

Soviet Ministry of Defense. <u>Whence the Threat to Peace?</u>, 2d ed. Moscow: Soviet Ministry of Defense, 1982.

Steele, Jonathan. "The Soviet View of National Security." In: <u>Soviet Power</u>. New York: Simon and Schuster, 1983, pp. 15-25.

Strode, Dan L., and Rebecca V. Strode. "Diplomacy and Defense in Soviet National Security Policy." <u>International Security</u> 7 (Fall 1983): 91-117. (2)

Tucker, Robert W. "Toward a New Detente." <u>New York Times Magazine</u>, October 9, 1984.

US Department of Defense. <u>Soviet Military Power</u>. Washington DC: Government Printing Office, annual. (2)

Wells, Samuel F., Jr. "Sounding the Tocsin: NSC 68 and the Soviet Threat." <u>International Security</u> 4 (Fall 1979): 116-58.

White, Ralph K. "Emphasizing with the Rule of the USSR." <u>Political Psychology</u> 4 (March 1983): 121-137.

Windass, Stan. <u>The Rite of War</u>. London: Pergamon, 1986, pp. 1-45.

CONFLICT MANAGEMENT:

This section includes discussions of institutions and methods of conflict management with reference to international organizations (e.g. U.N.), alternative security arrangements, diplomacy, nonalignment, nonviolence, negotiation (other than arms control treaties, found under the section on Arms Control below), peace research, and war termination.

Acheson, Dean. <u>Present at the Creation.</u> New York: Norton, 1971. pp. 478-85, 513-17.

Axelrod, Robert. <u>The Evolution of Cooperation</u>. New York: Basic Books, 1984. (2)

Bernstein, Barton J. "The Week We Almost Went to War." <u>Bulletin of Atomic Scientists</u> 32 (February 1976): 13-21.

Boulding, Elise. "Directory of Selected International Nongovernmental Associations with Membership Units in Nicaragua, Listed by Type of Organizational Activity." Yearbook of International Organizations, 1986-1987, 3d ed., vol. 2. Edited by Union of International Associations. New York: K.G. Saur, 1987.

Boulding, Kenneth E. National Defense Through Stable Peace. Laxenburg, Austria: International Institute for Applied Systems Analysis, 1983.

Boulding, Kenneth E. "Nongovernmental Organizations." Bulletin of the Atomic Scientists. (August 1985): 94-96.

Boulding, Kenneth E. Stable Peace. Austin, TX: University of Texas Press, 1978.

Bracken Paul, "Accidental Nuclear War." In: Hawks, Doves, and Owls, pp. 37-53. Edited by Graham T. Allison, Albert Carnesale, and Joseph S. Nye. New York: W.W. Norton, 1985.

Cox, Gray. The Ways of Peace: A Philosophy of Peace as Action. Mahwah, NJ: Paulist Press, 1986.

Deutsch, M. "Preventing World War III: A Pychological Perspective." Political Psychology 4 (1983): 3-32.

Drummond, Roscoe and Gaston Coblentz. Duel at the Brink. New York: Doubleday, 1984.

Falk, Richard, S.S. Kim, and S.H. Mendlovitz, eds. Toward A Just World Order. Boulder, CO: Westview Press, 1982.

Fisher, Roger. International Conflict for Beginners. New York: Harper & Row, 1969. Pp. 104-54.

Fisher, Roger, and William Ury. Getting to Yes. New York: Penguin Books, 1981.

Gandhi, Mohandas K. "On Nonviolence." In: Peace and War. Edited by Charles R. Beitz and Theodore Herman, pp. 345-48. San Francisco: Freeman & Co., 1973

Geertz, Clifford. The Interpretation of Cultures. New York: Basic Books, 1973.

Bibliography

Gould, Stephen. <u>The Flamingo's Smile: Reflections in Natural History</u>. New York: Norton, 1987.

Halloran, Richard. "The Game is War, and It's for Keeps." <u>New York Times</u>, June 1, 1987, p. 10.

Harris, Marvin. <u>Cannibals and Kings: The Origins of Culture</u>. New York: Random, 1978.

Hart, B.H. Liddell. "Aggression and the Problem of Weapons." <u>English Review</u> (July 1932): 71-78.

Hilsman, Roger, and Ronald Steel. "An Exchange of Views." <u>New York Review of Books</u>, May 8, 1969, pp. 36-38.

Hoag, Malcolm. "On Stability in Deterrent Races." <u>World Politics</u> 14 (July 1961): 505-527.

Ikle, Fred Charles. <u>Every War Must End</u>. New York: Columbia University Press, 1971.

Kahler, Miles. "Rumors of War: The 1914 Analogy." <u>Foreign Affairs</u> 58 (1980): 374-96. (2)

Kennedy, Robert. <u>Thirteen Days: A Memoir of the Cuban Missile Crisis</u>. New York: Norton, 1969. (2)

Keohane, Robert, and Joseph Nye. "Realism and Complex Interdependence." In: <u>Power and Interdependence</u>, pp. 23-37. Boston: Little, Brown, 1977.

King, Martin Luther, Jr. <u>Stride Toward Freedom</u>. New York: Harper, 1958.

Jervis, Robert. "Cooperation Under the Security Dilemma." <u>World Politics</u> 30 (1978): 167-214. (3)

Knightley, Philip. <u>The First Casualty: The War Correspondent as Hero, Propogandist, and Myth Maker</u>. San Diego: Harcourt, Brace, Jovanovich, 1976. pp. 79-113.

Konner, Melvin. <u>The Tangled Wing: Biological Constraints on the Human Spirit</u>. New York: Harper-Row, 1983.

Lebow, Richard Nedd. "A Research Agenda for Peace and Security Studies." <u>PS</u> 20 (Spring 1987): 252-57.

Lebow, Richard Nedd. "Is Crisis Management Always Possible?" Political Science Quarterly 102 (Summer 1987): 181-92.

Lebow, Richard Nedd. "The Cuban Missile Crisis: Reading the Lessons Correctly." Political Science Quarterly 98 (1983): 431-58.

Leng, Russell. "Coercive Bargaining in Recurrent Crises." Journal of Conflict Resolution 27 (1983): 379-419.

Luck, Edward C. "The UN at 40: A Supporter's Lament." Foreign Policy 57 (Winter 1984/85): 143-59.

Nathan, James A. "The Missile Crisis: His Finest Hour Now." World Politics 27 (1975): 85-6.

Nye, Joseph S., Jr. "Nuclear Risk Reduction Measures and U.S.--Soviet Relations." In: Preventing Nuclear War, pp. 7-23. Edited by Barry Blechman. Bloomington, IN: Indiana University Press, 1985.

Osgood, C.E. "Reciprocal Initiative." In: The Liberal Papers," pp. 155-228. Edited by J. Roosevelt. Chicago: Quadrangle Press, 1962.

Rusk, Dean, et al. "The Lessons of the Cuban Missile Crisis." Time, September 27 1982, pp. 85-6.

Schelling, Thomas C. "Confidence in Crisis." International Security 8 (Spring 1984): 55-66.

Schelling, Thomas. The Strategy of Conflict. Cambridge, MA: Harvard University Press, 1960. Appendix A, Part IV. (2)

Scott, Peter Dale. "Introductory Essay." In: Peace and World Order Studies, pp. 4-15. Edited by Barbara J. Wein. New York: World Policy Institute, 1984.

Sharp, Gene. "Types of Principled Nonviolence." In: Gandhi as a Political Strategist, pp. 201-34. Boston: Porter Sargent, 1979.

Smoke, Richard, and William Ury. Beyond the Hotline: Controlling a Nuclear Crisis. Cambridge, MA: Nuclear Negotiation Project, Harvard Law School, 1984.

Bibliography

Snyder, Jack L. "Rationality at the Brink: The Role of Cognitive Processes in Failures of Deterrence." World Politics 30 (April 1978): 345-365.

Stoessinger, John. "Preserving Peace in the State System." In: Games Nations Play, 6th ed, pp. 575-98. Washington, DC: CQ Press, 1987.

Sweeney, Duane, ed. The Peace Catalog. Seattle: Press for Peace, 1984.

Walton, Richard, and Robert McKersie, eds. A Behavioral Theory of Labor Negotiations. New York: McGraw Hill, 1965. Pp. 126-183.

Will, George. "The Lessons of the Cuban Crisis." Newsweek, October 11, 1982, p. 120.

STRATEGIC DOCTRINE:

This section includes discussions of deterrence, retaliation, mutual assured destruction, war planning, fighting, and avoidance, with reference to targeting of nuclear weapons, escalation, and grand strategy.

Abrams, Elliot. "Deterrence as Moral Response." Society 20 (September/October 1983): 26-29.

Adelman, Kenneth. "Beyond MAD-ness." Policy Review 17 (Summer 1981): 77-85.

Aldridge, Robert C. The Counterforce Syndrome: A Guide to Nuclear Weapons and Strategic Doctrine. Washington, DC: Institute for Policy Studies, 1978. (2)

Aldridge, Robert C. First Strike! The Pentagon's Strategy for Nuclear War. Boston: South End Press, 1982.

Alperovitz, Gar. Cold War Essays. Cambridge, MA: Schenkman, 1970. Pp. 51-73.

Alperovitz, Gar. Atomic Diplomacy: Hiroshima and Potsdam. New York: Penguin, 1985.

Arkin, William. Research Guide to Current Military and Strategic Affairs. Washington, DC: Institute for Policy Studies, 1981.

Arnatt, Robert. "Soviet Attitudes Toward Nuclear War: Do They Really Think They Can Win?" _Journal of Strategic Studies_ 2 (September 1979): 172-92. (3)

Art, Robert J. "Between Assured Destruction and Nuclear Victory: The Case for the 'MAD-plus' Posture." _Ethics_ 95 (April 1985): 497-516.

Baldwin, David. "The Power of Positive Sanctions." _World Politics_ 24 (1971): 119-38.

Ball, Desmond. "Counterforce Targeting: How New? How Viable?" _Arms Control Today_ 11 (February 1981): 1-2, 6-9. (2)

Ball, Desmond. _Targeting for Strategic Deterrence_. Adelphi Paper 185. London: International Institute for Strategic Studies. 1983. (2)

Ball, Desmond. "US Strategic Forces: How Would They Be Used?" _International Security_ 7 (1982-83): 31-60.

Barnet, Richard J. _Real Security: Restoring American Power in a Dangerous Decade_. New York: Simon and Schuster, 1981. (2)

Barnet, Richard J. "Ritual Dance of the Superpowers." _The Nation_, April 9, 1983, pp. 448-56.

Berkowitz, Bruce D. "Technological Progress, Strategic Weapons, and American Nuclear Policy." _Orbis_ 29 (1985): 241-258.

Bernstein, Barton J. "Doomsday II." _New York Times Magazine_, July 27, 1975, p. 106.

Bernstein, Barton J. "New Light on the A-Bomb Race." _The Nation_, September 16, 1978, pp. 238-42.

Betts, Richard. "Compound Deterrence versus No-First-Use: What's Wrong is What's Right." _Orbis_ 28 (Winter 1985): 697-718.

Betts, Richard. "Nuclear Surprise Attack: Deterrence, Defense and Conceptual Contradictions in American Policy." _Jerusalem Journal of International Relations_ 5 (1981): 82-89.

Bibliography

Blackett, Patrick M.. <u>Studies of War: Nuclear and Conventional</u>. Westport CT: Greenwood Press, 1962.

Blair, Bruce. <u>Strategic Command and Control</u>. Washington, DC: Brookings, 1985.

Blechman, Barry, and Stephen Kaplan. <u>Force Without War.</u> Washington DC: Brookings, 1978.

Bottome, Edgar. <u>The Balance of Terror: Nuclear Weapons and the Illusion of Security in the Nuclear Age, 1945-85</u>. Boston: Beacon Press, 1986.

Bracken, Paul. "Unintended Consequences of Strategic Gaming." <u>Simulation and Games</u> 8 (1977): 283-318.

Bracken, Paul, and Martin Shubik. "Strategic War: What Are the Questions and Who Should Answer Them?" <u>Technology and Society</u> 4 (1982): 155-179.

Brodie, Bernard. <u>Escalation and the Nuclear Option.</u> Ann Arbor, MI: Books on Demand, n.d.

Brodie, Bernard. <u>Strategy in the Missile Age</u>. Princeton, NJ: Princeton University Press, 1959. (3)

Carter, Barry. "Nuclear Strategy and Nuclear Weapons." <u>Scientific American</u>, May 1974, pp. 20-31.

Center for Defense Information. "First Strike Weapons at Sea." <u>Defense Monitor</u> 16 (1987): 1-8.

Center for Defense Information. "Preparing for Nuclear War: President Reagan's Program." <u>Defense Monitor</u> 10 (1982): 1-6, 14-16.

Chomsky, Noam. <u>For Reasons of State.</u> New York: Pantheon Books, 1978.

Coalition for a New Foreign and Military Policy. "Anti-Submarine Warfare." <u>First Strike Paper</u>. Washington, DC: Coalition for a New Foreign and Military Policy, 1986. 4pp.

DeGrasse, Robert, Jr., P. Murphy, and W. Ragen. <u>The Costs and Consequences of Reagan's Military Buildup</u>. New York: Council on Economic Priorities, 1982. (2)

"Denuclearization for a Just World: The Failure of Non-Proliferation." Alternatives 6 (1980-81): 491-96.

Draper, Theodore. "How Not to Think About Nuclear War." New York Review of Books, July 15, 1982, pp. 35-43.

Dunn, Keith, and William Staudenmaier. "Strategy for Survival." Foreign Policy 52 (Fall 1983): 22-41.

Earle, Edward M., ed. Makers of Modern Strategy: Military Thought from Machiavelli to Hitler. Princeton, NJ: Princeton University Press, 1943.

Epstein, Joshua. "Horizontal Escalation: Sour Notes of a Recurrent Theme." International Security 8 (Winter 1983-84): 19-31.

Erickson, John. "The Soviet View of Deterrence." Survival 26 (1984): 242-51.

Etzold, Thomas, and John Gaddis, eds. Containment: Documents on American Policy and Strategy, 1945-50. New York: Columbia University Press, 1978.

Falk, Richard. Legal Order in A Violent World. Princeton, NJ: Princeton University Press, 1969. Chaps. 12-14.

Fletcher, Keyworth, Sidney Drell, and Wolfgang Panofsky. "Symposium on Ballistic Missile Defense." Issues in Science and Technology 1 (Fall 1984): 15-65.

Forsberg, Randall. "A Bilateral Nuclear Weapons Freeze." Scientific American, November 1982. (5)

Freedman, Lawrence. The Evolution of Nuclear Strategy. New York: St. Martin, 1981. (2)

Friedberg, Aaron L. "A History of US Strategic 'Doctrine', 1945 to 1980." Journal of Strategic Studies 3 (December 1980): 37-71. (2)

Garthoff, Raymond, and Richard Pipes. "A Garthoff-Pipes Debate on Soviet Strategic Doctrine." Strategic Review 10 (Fall 1982): 36-63.

Bibliography

George, Alexander, and Richard Smoke. Deterrence in American Foreign Policy: Theory and Practice. New York: Colombia University Press, 1974. (3)

Glennon, John P. Foreign Relations of the US, 1951. vol 1. Washington, DC: Government Printing Office, 1960. pp. 163-78, 180-81. (2)

Gooch, G. P. and Harold Temperley, eds. "Crowe and Sanderson Memoranda." British Documents on the Origins of the War, Vol. 1, pp. 397-431. New York: Johnson Reprint Corporation.

Gray, Colin. "Defense Planning and the Duration of War." Defense Analysis 1 (1985): 21-36.

Gray, Colin. "Nuclear Strategy: A Case for a Theory of Victory." International Security 4 (1979): 54-87.

Gray, Colin. Nuclear Strategy and Strategic Planning. Philadelphia: Foreign Policy Research Institute, 1984.

Gray, Colin. "Strategic Stability Reconsidered: US Defense Policy in the 1980s." Daedalus 109 (1980): 135-54. (2)

Gray, Colin. Strategic Studies and Public Policy: The American Experience. Lexington, KY: University Press of Kentucky, 1982.

Gray, Colin. "War Fighting for Deterrence." Journal of Strategic Studies 7 (1984): 5-28. (2)

Gray, Colin, and Keith Payne. "Victory is Possible." Foreign Policy 39 (Summer 1980): 14-27.

Haldeman, H.R. The Ends of Power. New York: Dell, 1978. Pp. 117-24, 139-40.

Halperin, Morton. "The Lessons Nixon Learned." In: The Legacy of Vietnam and the Future of Foreign Policy, pp. 411-28. Edited by Anthony Lake. New York: New York University Press, 1976.

Hewlett, Richard, and Oscar Anderson. The New World. College Park, PA: Pennsylvania State University Press, 1962.

Hoffman, Stanley. Duties Beyond Borders: On the Limits and Possibilities of International Politics. Syracuse, NY: Syracuse University Press, 1981. pp.45-93. (2)

Holdren, John P. "SDI, the Soviets, and the Prospects for Arms Control," pp. 189-205. In: Strategic Defense and the Western Alliance. Edited by Sanfcrd Lakoff and Randy Willoughby. Lexington, MA: Lexington Books, 1987.

Holloway, David. "Military Power and Political Purpose in Soviet Society." Daedalus 109 (1980): 13-30.

Howard, Michael. The Classical Strategists. Adelphi Paper 54. London: International Institute for Strategic Studies, 1969. Pp. 18-32.

Howard, Michael. Clausewitz. New York: Oxford University Press, 1983.

Howard, Michael. "On Fighting Nuclear War." International Security 5 (1980): 3-17.

Howard, Michael. "An Incredible Strategy." New York Review of Books 28 (1982): 12.

Huntington, Samuel. "Conventional Deterrence and Conventional Retaliation in Europe." International Security 8 (Winter 1983-84): 32-56.

Hull, Paul, and Bruce Russett. "What Makes Deterrence Work? Cases from 1900 to 1980." World Politics 36 (July 1984): 497-526.

Ikle, Fred Charles. "Can Nuclear Deterrence Last Out the Century." Foreign Affairs 51 (July 1973): 267-85. (2)

Ikle, Fred Charles. "The Reagan Program: A Focus on the Strategic Imperatives." Strategic Review 10 (1982): 11-18.

Independent Commission on International Development Issues. North-South: A Programme for Survival. Edited by Willy Brandt and Anthony Sampson. Cambridge, MA: MIT Press, 1980. pp. 117-25.

Bibliography

Jervis, Robert. "Bargaining and Bargaining Tactics." In: Coercion, pp. 272-288. Edited by J. Roland Pennock and John Chapmen. Brooklyn NY: Lieber-Atherton, 1972.

Jervis, Robert. "Deterrence and Perception." International Security 7 (Winter 1982-83): 3-31. (2)

Jervis, Robert. "Deterrence Theory Revisited." World Politics 31 (1979): 289-324. (3)

Jervis, Robert. The Illogic of American Nuclear Strategy. Ithaca, NY: Cornell University Press, 1985. Chap. 1-6.

Jervis, Robert. "Why Nuclear Superiority Doesn't Matter." Political Science Quarterly 94 (1979-80). (2)

Jervis, Robert, et al. Psychology and Deterrence. Baltimore: Johns Hopkins University Press, 1985.

Kahn, Herman. Thinking About the Unthinkable in the 1980's. New York: Simon and Schuster, 1984. (4)

Kaiser, Karl, et al. "Nuclear Weapons and the Preservation of Peace." Foreign Affairs 60 (Spring 1982): 753-768.

Kaiser, Robert, and Walter Pincus. "The Doomsday Debate: Shall We Attack America?" Washington Post, August 12, 1979, p. B-1.

Kaku, M., and J. Trainer. Nuclear Power: Both Sides. New York: Norton, 1982.

Kalb, Marvin, and Bernard Kalb. Kissinger. Boston: Little and Brown, 1974.

Kaplan, Fred. "Strategic Thinkers." Bulletin of Atomic Scientists (December 1982): 51-56.

Kennan, George F. "A Modest Proposal." New York Review of Books, July 16, 1981, p. 14.

Kennedy, Paul. "America Takes a Giant Step Backward." New Society May 20, 1982, pp. 293-94.

Kennedy, Paul. The Rise and Fall of British Naval Mastery. Melbourne, FL: Krieger, 1982.

Kenny, Anthony. The Logic of Deterrence. Chicago: University of Chicago Press, 1985. (2)

Komer, Robert. "Maritime Strategy vs. Coalition Defense." Foreign Affairs 60 (Summer 1982): 1124-44.

Knorr, K. "On the Military Uses of Military Force in the Contemporary World." Orbis 21 (1977): 5-27.

Lebow, Richard Nedd. Between Peace and War. Baltimore: Johns Hopkins University Press, 1981. pp. 148-228.

Legvold, Robert. "Strategic Doctrine and SALT: Soviet and American Views." Survival 21 (January/February 1979): 8-13.

Lehman, John. "Rebirth of a US Naval Strategy." Strategic Review 9 (1981): 9-15.

Lewis, John. "China's Military Doctrines and Force Posture." In: China's Quest for Independence: Policy Evolution In the 1970's, pp. 147-98. Edited by Thomas Fingar. Boulder, CO: Westview Press, 1980.

Luttwak, Edward. The Grand Strategy of the Soviet Union. New York: St. Martin's, 1985.

Luttwak, Edward. "How to Think About Nuclear War." Commentary, August 1982, pp. 21-28. (2)

Magruder, Jeb Stewart. An American Life: One Man's Road to Watergate. New York: Atheneum, 1974. Pp. 92-98.

Masters, Dexter, and Katherine Way. One World or None. New York: McGraw-Hill, 1948.

McNamara, Robert. "The Military Role of Nuclear Weapons: Perceptions and Misperceptions." Foreign Affairs 62 (1983): 59-80. (2)

Mahan, Alfred Thayer. The Influence of Sea Power upon History, 1660-1783. New York: Little and Brown, 1890, pp. 1-77.

Marshall, George C., Jr. "A Postwar Military Establishment." In: The American Way of War: A History of

Bibliography

US Military Strategy and Policy, pp. 55-58. Edited by Russell F. Weigley. Bloomington, IN: Indiana University Press, 1977. (2)

Mearsheimer, John J. Conventional Deterrence. Ithaca, NY: Cornell University Press, 1985.

Medvedev, Roy, and Zhores Medvedev. "Nuclear Samizdat." The Nation, January 16, 1982, pp. 13-23.

Miller, Marc S. "Ambiguous War: The United States and Low Intensity Conflict." Technology Review (August/September 1987): 60-67.

Miller, Mark E. Soviet Strategic Power and Doctrine: The Quest for Superiority. Miami: Advanced International Studies Institute, 1982, pp. 208-227.

Miller, Steven E., ed. Military Strategy and the Origins of World War I: An International Security Reader. Princeton, NJ: Princeton University Press, 1985.

Milstein, M.A. and L.S. Semeiko. "Problems of the Inadmissibility of Nuclear Conflict." International Studies Quarterly 20 (1976): 87-103. Translated by Philip D. Stewart.

Morris, Roger. Uncertain Greatness: Henry Kissinger and American Foreign Policy. New York: Harper and Row, 1977. Pp. 163-71.

Myrdal, Alva. The Game of Disarmament. New York: Pantheon, 1982. Pp.23-65.

Newman, James R., ed. The World of Mathematics. vol 4. New York: Simon and Schuster, 1956. pp. 2138-57.

Nitze, Paul. "Assuring Strategic Stability in an Era of Detente." Foreign Affairs 54 (1976): 207-32. (4)

Nitze, Paul. "Deterring Our Deterrent." Foreign Policy 25 (Winter 1976-77): 195-210.

Nixon, Richard. RN: The Memoirs of Richard Nixon. New York: Grosset and Dunlap, 1978.

Panofsky, Wolfgang K.H. "The Mutual Hostage Relationship Between America and Russia." In: Nuclear Strategy and National Security: Points of View, pp. 74-83. Edited by Robert J. Pranger and Roger Labrie. Washington, DC: American Enterprise Institute, 1977. (2)

Porro, Jeffrey D. "The Policy War: Brodie vs. Kahn." Bulletin of Atomic Scientists 38 (June/July 1982): 16-19.

Posen, Barry R. The Sources of Military Doctrine: France, Britain, and Germany Between the World Wars. Ithaca, NY: Cornell University Press, 1971.

Posen, Barry R., and Stephen W. Van Evera. "Reagan Administration Defense Policy: Departure from Containment." In: Eagle Defiant: American Foreign Policy in the 1980's, pp. 67-104. Edited by Kenneth A. Oye, Robert J. Lieber and Donald Rothchild. Boston: Little and Brown, 1983.

Powers, Thomas M. "Choosing a Strategy for World War III." Atlantic, November, 1982, pp. 82-110.

Quester, George. Deterrence Before Hiroshima. New Brunswick, NJ: Transaction Books, 1986.

Rapoport, Anatol. "Lewis Richardson's Mathematical Theory of War." Journal of Conflict Resolution 72 (September 1957): 275-98.

Reagan, Ronald. "Address to the Nation." New York Times, November 23, 1982.

Record, Jeffrey. "Jousting with Unreality: Reagan's Military Strategy." International Security 8 (1983-84): 3-18.

Richelson, Jeffrey. "PD-59, NSDD-13 and the Reagan Strategic Modernization Program." Journal of Strategic Studies 6 (June 1983): 125-46.

Rosenberg, David Alan. "The American Atomic Strategy and the Hydrogen Bomb Decision." Journal of American History 66 (June 1979): 62-87. (3)

Rosenberg, David Alan. "'A Smoking Radiating Ruin at the End of Two Hours:' Documents on American Plans for Nuclear War with the Soviet Union, 1954-55." International Security 6 (1981-82): 3-17. (2)

Bibliography

Rothschild, Emma. "The Delusions of Deterrence." New York Review of Books, April 14, 1983, pp. 40-50.

Rowen, Henry S. "The Evolution of Strategic Nuclear Doctrine." In: Strategic Thought in the Nuclear Age, pp.131-56. Edited by Laurence Martin. Baltimore: Johns Hopkins, 1979. (2)

Rowen, Henry, and Albert Wohlstetter. "Varying Response with Circumstance." In: Beyond Nuclear Deterrence: New Aims, New Arms, pp. 225-38. Edited by Johan Holst and Uwe Nerlich. New York: Crane Russak, 1977.

Russett, Bruce. "Refining Deterrence Theory: The Japanese Attack on Pearl Harbor." In: Theory and Research on the Causes of War. Edited by Dean G. Pruitt and Richard C. Snyder. Englewood Cliffs NJ: Prentice-Hall, 1969.

Sailager, F.M. "The Road to Total War: Escalation in World War II." Rand Report R-455-FR. Palo Alto, CA: Rand Institute, April 1960.

Schelling, Thomas C., Leon Sloss, and Randall Forsberg. "Abolition of Ballistic Missiles." International Security 12 (Summer 1987): 179-96.

Schilling, Warner. "US Strategic Nuclear Concepts in the 1970's: The Search for Sufficiently Equivalent Countervailing Parity." International Security 6 (1981): 49-79.

Schwartz, David. NATO's Nuclear Dilemmas. Washington, DC: Brookings, 1983. Pp. 136-251.

Scoville, Herbert, Jr. "America's Greatest Construction: Can It Work?" New York Review of Books, March 20, 1980, pp. 12-17.

Shearer, Derek. "The Pentagon Propaganda Machine." In: The Pentagon Watchers: Students Report on the National Security State, pp. 99-142. Edited by Leonard Rodberg and Derek Shearer. New York: Doubleday, 1970.

Sigal, Leon. "Rethinking the Unthinkable." Foreign Policy 34 (Spring 1979): 35-51.

Sloss, Leon, and Marc Millott. "US Nuclear Strategy in Evolution." Strategic Review 12 (1984): 19-28.

Smoke, Richard. War: Controlling Escalation. Cambridge, MA: Harvard University Press, 1978. pp. 19-48, 195-236, 268-97.

Snow, C.P. Science and Government. Cambridge, MA: Harvard University Press, 1961. pp. 47-53.

Snyder, Glenn. "The Balance of Power and the Balance of Terror." In: The Balance of Power. Edited by Paul Seabury. San Francisco: Chandler Press, 1965. (2)

Snyder, Glenn. Deterrence and Defence: Toward a Theory of National Security. Princeton, NJ: Princeton University Press, 1961. pp. 1-16.

Speed, Roger. Strategic Deterrence in the 1980's. Palo Alto, CA: Hoover Institution, 1979.

Stegenda, James A. "Nuclear Deterrence: Bankrupt Ideology." Policy Sciences 16 (1983): 127-145.

Summers, Harry. On Strategy: A Critical Analysis of the Vietnam War. Novato, CA: Presidio Press, 1982.

Szulc, Tad, and Stephen Orgel. The Illusion of Power. Berkeley, CA: University of California Press, 1974. Pp. 148-56.

Taumen, Ronald L. "The Reagan Strategic Program." Arms Control Today 11 (1981): 1-3, 5-6.

Taylor, A.J. The Origins of the Second World War. New York: Atheneum, 1983.

Thompson, E.P. Beyond the Cold War: A New Approach to the Arms Race and Nuclear Annihilation. New York: Pantheon Books, 1982. (2)

Trachtenberg, Marc. "The Influence of Nuclear Weapons in the Cuban Missile Crisis." International Security 10 (Summer 1985): 137-93.

Trofimenko, Henry. Changing Attitudes Toward Deterrence. Working Paper No. 25. Los Angeles: Center for International and Strategic Affairs, University of California--Los Angeles, 1980.

Bibliography

Tuchman, Barbara. _The Guns of August_. New York: Mac-Millan, 1962.

Tuchman, Barbara. _The Proud Tower_, New York: Mac-Millan, 1966., chap. 5. (2)

Turner, Stanisfield, and George George. "Preparing for the Unexpected: The Need for a New Military Strategy." _Foreign Affairs_ 61 (Fall 1982): 122-135.

Ullman, Richard E. "Redefining Security." _International Security_ 8 (Summer 1983): 129-153. (2)

Ullman, Richard H. "No First Use of Nuclear Weapons." _Foreign Affairs_ 50 (July 1972): 669-83.

US Department of Defense. _The Reagan Strategic Program_. Washington, DC: Government Printing Office, 1981.

US Executive Office of the President, National Security Advisor. _Details of National Security Strategy_. June 16, 1982, pp. 1-17.

US National Security Council. "US Objectives with Respect to Russia." NSC Document 20/1, 1948. In: _Containment: Documents on American Policy and Strategy, 1945-50_. Edited by Thomas Etzold and John Gaddis. New York: Columbia University Press, 1978.

US National Security Council. NSC Document 168/1. In: _Foreign Relations of the US, 1952-54_, 2 (1954): 567-76.

Virilio, Paul, and Sylvere Lotringer. _Pure War_. New York: Semiotext, 1983. (2)

Waltz, Kenneth. "What Will the Spread of Nuclear Weapons Do to the World?" In: _International Political Effects of the Spread of Nuclear Weapons_, pp. 165-94. Edited by John Kerry King. Washington, DC: Government Printing Office, 1979.

Weigley, Russell F. _The American Way of War: A History of US Military Strategy and Policy_. Bloomington, IN: Indiana University Press, 1977. (2)

Weigley, Russell F. Eisenhower's Lieutenants: The Campaigns of France and Germany, 1944-1945. Bloomington, IN: Indiana University Press, 1981. pp. 1-55, 77-95, 114-143.

Wells, Samuel F. Jr. "The Origins of Massive Retaliation". Political Science Quarterly 96 (Spring 1981): 31-53. (2)

Williams, John. "US Navy Missions and Force Structure: A Critical Reappraisal." Armed Forces and Society 7 (1981): 499-528.

Wohlstetter, Albert. "Between an Unfree World and None: Increasing our Choices." Foreign Affairs 63 (Summer 1985): 962-994.

Wohlstetter, Albert. "The Delicate Balance of Terror." Foreign Affairs 37 (January 1959): 211-234. (4)

Yergen, Daniel. Shattered Peace. Boston: Houghton and Mifflin, 1977.

York, Herbert R. "Toward a Balance of Terror." In: Race to Oblivion: A Participant's View of the Arms Race. New York: Simon and Schuster, 1970. Part I, pp. 9-48, 156-239. (2)

Yost, David. "French Nuclear Targeting." In: Strategic Nuclear Targeting. Edited by Desmond Ball and Jeffrey Richelson. Ithaca, NY: Cornell University Press, 1986.

Young, Robert J. In Command of France: French Foreign Policy and Military Planning, 1933-40. Cambridge, MA: Harvard University Press, 1978. pp. 1-12, 221-58.

ARMS CONTROL:

This section includes discussions of the history, economics, politics, and future of arms control and disarmament efforts concerning both nuclear and conventional weapons, with reference to negotiation of specific treaties, attitudes of governments and citizens toward them, and proposals for a nuclear freeze

Adelman, Kenneth. "Arms Control With and Without Agreements." Foreign Affairs 63 (Winter 1984-85): 240-63. (2)

Bibliography

American Friends Service Committee. "Mapping Kit." New York: American Friends Service Committee, 1981.

Arms Control Association. <u>A Glossary of Arms Control Terms</u>. Washington, DC: Carnegie Endowment for International Peace, 1979.

Arms Control Association. <u>Arms Control and National Security: An Introduction</u>. Washington, DC: Arms Control Association, 1983.

Aspin, Les. "The Verification of the SALT II Agreement." <u>Scientific American</u>, February 1979, pp. 38-45. (3)

Ball, Desmond. <u>Can Nuclear War Be Controlled</u>? Adelphi Paper 169. London: International Institute for Strategic Studies, 1981.

Barnaby, Frank. "The Mounting Prospects of Nuclear War." <u>Bulletin of Atomic Scientists</u> 33 (June 1977): 11-19.

Barnet, Richard J. <u>Global Reach</u>. New York: Simon and Schuster, 1974.

Barnet, Richard J. "Ritual Dance of the Superpowers." <u>The Nation</u>, April 9, 1983, pp. 448-50.

Barton, John, and Ryukichi Imai. <u>Arms Control II: A New Approach to International Security</u>. Boston: Oelgeshlager, Gunn, and Hain, 1981.

Bay, Christian. "Hazards of Goliath in the Nuclear Age: Need for Rational Priorities in American Peace and Defense Policies." <u>Alternatives: A Journal of World Policy</u> 8 (1983): 501-542.

Bernstein, Barton J. "The Challenges and Dangers of Nuclear Weapons: American Foreign Policy and Strategy." <u>Foreign Service</u> Journal (September 1978). (2)

Bertram, Christopher. <u>The Future of Arms Control Part I, Beyond SALT II</u>. Adelphi Paper 141. London: International Institute of Strategic Studies, 1980.

Bertram, Christopher. <u>The Future of Arms Control Part II, Arms Control and Technological Change: Elements of</u>

a New Approach. Adelphi Paper 146. London: International Institute of Strategic Studies, 1980.

Betts, Richard. "Nuclear Weapons." In: The Making of America's Soviet Policy, pp. 97-127. Edited by Joseph Nye, Jr. New Haven: Yale University Press, 1984.

Betts, Richard. "The Tragicomedy of Arms Trade Control." International Security 5 (Summer 1980): 80-110.

Biden, Joseph. "The Necessity of Arms Control." Remarks to the Arms Control Association, December 12, 1979.

Blacker, Coit, and Gloria Duffy, eds. International Arms Control: Issues and Agreements, 2d ed. Palo Alto, CA: Stanford University Press, 1984. (5)

Blechman, Barry M. "Do Negotiated Arms Limitations Have a Future?" Foreign Affairs 58 (Fall 1980): 120-125. (3)

Blechman, Barry, and Alton Quanbeck. "The Arms Accord: Everyone Gains." Washington Post, 14 June 1972.

Boston Study Group. Winding Down. New York: W.H. Freeman, 1982.

Boyer, Paul. "From Activism to Apathy: The American People and Nuclear Weapons, 1963-1980." Journal of American History 70 (1984): 821-844.

Brennan, Donald G. "When the SALT Hits the Fan." National Review, June 23, 1972, pp. 685-92.

Bresler, Robert J. "The Tangled Politics of SALT." Arms Control (May 1982): 1-12.

Bresler, Robert J., and Robert C. Gray. "The Bargaining Chip and SALT." Political Science Quarterly 92 (Spring 1977): 65-88.

Brodie, Bernard. "On the Objectives of Arms Control." International Security 1 (1976): 17-36. (2)

Brown, Harold, and Lynn Davis. "Nuclear Arms Control: Where Do We Stand?" Foreign Affairs 62 (Summer 1984): 1145-1161.

Bibliography

Bull, Hedley. "Arms Control and World Order." International Security 1 (Summer 1976): 3-16.

Bull, Hedley. "Strategic Arms Limitations: The Prece-
dent of the Washington and London Naval Treaties." In:
Salt: Problems and Prospects, pp. 26-52. Edited by
Morton A. Kaplan. Morristown, NJ: General Learning
Press, 1973.

Bundy, McGeorge. "Early Thoughts on Controlling the
Nuclear Arms Race: A Report to the Secretary of State,
January 1953." International Security 7 (Fall 1982):
3-27.

Burt, Richard. "The Future of Arms Control...Or Half
Empty." Foreign Policy 36 (Fall 1979): 34-48.

Burt, Richard. "The Relevance of Arms Control in the
1980's." Daedalus 110 (Winter 1981): 159-77.

Burt, Richard. "The Scope and Limits of SALT." Foreign Affairs 56 (July 1978): 751-770.

Carlton, David. "Great Britain and the Coolidge Naval
Disarmament Conference of 1927." Political Science
Quarterly 83 (December 1968): 573-598.

Carnesale, Albert, and Richard Haas, Superpower Arms
Control: Setting the Record Straight. Cambridge, MA:
Ballinger, 1987.

Carter, Jimmy. Keeping Faith: Memoirs of a President.
New York: Bantam, 1983. pp. 212-265.

Chari, P.R. "An Indian Reaction to US Nonproliferation
Policy." International Security 3 (Fall 1978): 57-61.

Chayes, Abram. "An Inquiry into the Workings of Arms
Control Agreements." Harvard Law Review (March 1972):
905-969.

"China's Basic Position on Disarmament." Beijing Review, March 24, 1986, pp. 14-15.

Crown, J.R. " The Military Establishment: High Water
Mark?" Journal of International Affairs 26 (1972):
102-105.

Nuclear Weapons in the University Classroom

Cutler, Lloyd N., and Roger C. Molander. "Is There Life After Death in SALT?" International Security 6 (Fall 1981): 3-20.

Doty, Paul, and Robert Metzger. "Arms Control Enters the Gray Area." International Security 3 (Winter 1978): 17-52.

Drell, Sidney D. "Arms Control: Is There Still Hope?" Daedalus 109 (Fall 1980): 177-88.

Duffy, Gloria. "Crisis Mangling and the Cuban Brigade." International Security 7 (Summer 1983): 67-87.

Epstein, William. "A Ban on the Production of Fissionable Material for Weapons." Scientific American, July 1980, pp. 43-51.

Ermath, Fritz W. "Contrasts in American and Soviet Strategic Thought." International Security 3 (February 1978).

Evron, Yariv. The Role of Arms in the Middle East. Adelphi Paper 38. London: International Institute for Strategic Studies, 1967.

Falk, Richard. "Arms Control, Foreign Policy, and Global Reform." In: Arms, Defense Policy and Arms Control, pp.35-52. Edited by Franklin Long and George A. Rathjens. New York: Norton, 1976.

Feiveson, Harold. "Arms Control and Disarmament." In: The Future of the International Legal Order, vol. 3. Edited by Richard Falk and Cyril Black. Princeton, NJ: Princeton University Press, 1969.

Feiveson, Harold, and Frank Von Hipple. "The Freeze and the Counterforce Race." Physics Today, January 1983, pp. 36-49. (2)

Feld, Bernard T. "The Trouble with SALT." Saturday Review, October 1972, pp. 54-57.

Feldman, Shai. "The Bombing of Osiraq--Revisited." International Security 7 (Fall 1982): 114-142.

Feldman, Shai. "A Nuclear Middle East." Survival 23 (May-June 1981): 107-115.

Bibliography

Flanagan, Stephen J. "The Domestic Politics of SALT II: Implications for the Foreign Policy Process." In: Congress, The Presidency, and American Foreign Policy, pp. 44-77. Edited by J. Spanier and J. Nogee. New York: Pergamon Press, 1981.

Foelber, Robert. "The Limits of Arms Control." Backgrounder 280 (July 26, 1983): 1-15.

Forsberg, Randall. "Confining the Military to Defense as a Route to Disarmament." World Policy Journal (1984): 285-318.

Frye, Alton. "US Decision Making for SALT." In: Salt: The Moscow Agreements and Beyond, chap. 3. Edited by Mason Willrich. Free Press, 1974.

Garthoff, Raymond L. "Mutual Deterrence and Strategic Arms Limitation in Soviet Policy." International Security 3 (Summer 1978).

Garthoff, Raymond L. "Negotiating With the Russians: Some Lessons From SALT." International Security 1 (1977): 3-24. (2)

Garthoff, Raymond L. "On Estimating and Imputing Intentions." International Security 3 (Winter 1978): 23-32.

Garthoff, Raymond. "SALT I: An Evaluation." World Politics 31 (October 1978): 1-25.

Garwin, Richard. "Charged Particle Beam Weapons?" Bulletin of Atomic Scientists 34 (October 1978): 24-27.

Gelb, Leslie. "The Future of Arms Control...A Glass Half Full." Foreign Policy 36 (Fall 1979): 21-32.

George, Roger. "Salt and the Defense Budget." Arms Control Today 8 (November 1978): 1-4.

Gerber, Larry. "The Baruch Plan and the Origins of the Cold War." Diplomatic History (Winter 1982): 69-95.

Gilleland, Donald L. "The Perils of a Nuclear Freeze." Vital Speeches, June 15, 1983. pp. 514-517.

Gray, Colin S. "SALT I Aftermath: Have the Soviets Been Cheating?" Air Force Magazine, November 1975.

Hafemeister, D., et al. "The Verification of Compliance With Arms Control Agreements." Scientific American, March 1985, pp. 38-45.

Haley, P. Edward, et al. Nuclear Strategy: Arms Control and the Future. Boulder, CO: Westview Press, 1985. (2)

Hanreider, Wolfgang. Arms Control and Security: Current Issues. Boulder, CO: Westview Press, 1979.

Hassain, Farooq. Weapons Test Restrictions: A Means for Arms Control. Adelphi Paper 161. London: International Institute for Strategic Studies, 1981.

Holden, Constance. "Antinuclear Movement Gains Momentum" Science, Feb. 12, 1982, pp. 41-42.

Horelick, Arnold L., and Edward L. Warner III. "US-Soviet Nuclear Arms Control: The Next Phase," pp. 225-56. In: US-Soviet Relations: The Next Phase. Edited by Arnold L. Horelick. Ithaca, NY: Cornell University Press, 1986.

Ikenberry, John, and Michael Levine. "SALT and the Senate, Phase I." Arms Control Today 9 (September 1979).

Ikle, Fred Charles. "Arms Control and National Defense." In: The United States in the 1980's, pp. 419-33. Edited by Peter Duignan and Alvin Rabushka. Palo Alto, CA: Hoover Institution Press, 1980.

Imai, Ryukicki. "A Japanese Reaction to US Nonproliferation Policy." International Security 3 (Fall 1978): 62-66.

Johansen, Robert C. "Arms Bazaar: SALT was Never Intended to Disarm." Harpers, May 1979, p. 21.

Kagan, Robert W. "Why Arms Control Failed." Policy Review 27 (Winter 1984): 28-33.

Kaiser, Karl. "Nuclear Weapons and the Preservation of Peace: A German Response." Foreign Affairs 60 (1981-82): 1157-70. (2)

Bibliography

Kaldor, Mary. "Disarmament: The Armament Process in Reverse." In: Toward Nuclear Disarmament and Global Security: A Search for Alternatives, pp. 654-666. Edited by Burns H. Weston. Boulder: Westview Press, 1984.

Kelleher, Catherine M. "The Present as Prologue: Europe and Theatre Nuclear Modernization." International Security 6 (Summer 1981): 150-68.

Kemp, Jack F. "Congressional Expectations of SALT II." Strategic Review 7 (Winter 1979): 16-25.

Kintner, William R., and Robert L. Pfaltzgraff, Jr. "Assessing the Moscow SALT Arguments." Orbis 16 (1972): 341-360.

Klinger, Gil, and Herbert Scoville, Jr. "The Politics of START." Arms Control Today 12 (1982): 4-6.

Komer, Robert. "Maritime Strategy vs. Coalition Defense." Foreign Affairs 60 (Summer 1982): 1124-44.

Krass, Allan S. "The Politics of Verification." World Policy Journal 2 (Fall 1985): 731-51.

Krell, Gert. "The Problems and Achievements of Arms Control." Arms Control (December 1981): 247-83.

Krepon, Michael. "Assessing Strategic Arms Reduction Proposals." World Politics 36 (January 1983): 216-44.

Lackey, Douglas. "Disarmament Revisited: A Reply to Ravaka and Hardin." Philosophy and Public Affairs 12 (Summer 1983): 261-65.

Legvold, Robert. "Strategic Doctrine and SALT: Soviet and American Views." Survival 21 (January-February 1979): 8-13.

Levi, Barbara. "Directed Energy Weapons." Physics Today, August 1983. (2)

Lewis, John. "China's Military Doctrines and Force Posture." In: China's Quest for Independence: Policy Evolution In the 1970's, pp 147-98. Edited by Thomas Fingar. Boulder, CO: Westview Press, 1980.

Lodal, Jan M. "SALT II and American Security." Foreign Affairs 57 (1978): 245-68.

Long, Franklin A., and George W. Rathjens, eds. Arms, Defense Policy and Arms Control. New York: Norton, 1976.

Luttwak, Edward. "Why Arms Control Has Failed." Commentary, January 1978, pp. 19-28. (2)

McGraw, Kathleen M., and Tom R. Tyler. "The Threat of Nuclear War: Risk Interpretation and Behavioral Response." Journal of Social Issues 39 (1982): 25-40.

Miller, Steven E. "Politics Over Promise: Domestic Impediments to Arms Control." International Security 8 (Spring 1984): 67-90. (2)

Moynihan, Daniel P. "Reflections: The SALT Process." New Yorker, November 19, 1979, pp. 104-80.

Muravchik, Joshua. "The Perils of a Nuclear Freeze." World Affairs 145 (1982): 203-7.

Myers, Henry R. "Extending the Nuclear Test Ban." Scientific American 226 (January 1972): 13-23.

National Academy of Sciences. Nuclear Arms Control: Background and Issues. Washington, DC: National Academy Press, 1985. (2)

Neidle, Alan F. ed. Nuclear Negotiation: Reassessing Arms Control Goals in US-Soviet Relations. Austin, TX: Lyndon B. Johnson School of Public Affairs, 1982.

Newhouse, John. Cold Dawn: The Story of SALT. New York: Holt, Rinehart, and Winston, 1973.

Newhouse, John. "Reflections: The SALT Debate." New Yorker, December 17, 1979, pp. 130-66.

Nitze, Paul. Is SALT II a Fair Deal for the United States? Publication 14. N.p.: Committee on the Present Danger, 1979.

Nye, Joseph. "Farewell to Arms Control?" Foreign Affairs 64 (Fall 1986): 1-20.

Bibliography

Nye, Joseph. "Restarting Arms Control." Foreign Policy 47 (Summer 1982): 98-114.

Nye, Joseph. "Non-Proliferation: A Long-Term Strategy." Foreign Affairs 56 (April 1978): 601-23.

Orlander, D. "The Gas Centrifuge." Scientific American, August 1980. (2)

Osgood, Charles E. "A Case for Graduated Unilateral Disengagement." In: The Atomic Age, pp. 269-76. Edited by Morton Grodzins and Eugene Rabinowitz. New York: Basic Books, 1963.

Paine, Christopher. "The Freeze and the United Nations." Bulletin of Atomic Scientists (June/July 1982): 10-15.

Panofsky, Wolfgang. Arms Control and Salt II. Seattle: University of Washington Press, 1979.

Panovsky, Wolfgang. "Arms Control: Necessary Process." Bulletin of Atomic Scientists (March 1986): 35-38.

Pipes, Richard. Why the Soviet Union Wants SALT II. Publication 15. N.p: Committee on the Present Danger, 1979.

Placak, Bedrich, et al. "The Peace Movements in the East." Index on Censorship 13 (1984): 34-38.

Potter, William C. Verification and SALT. Boulder, CO: Westview Press, 1980. (2)

Ravaka, Gregory. "Doubts about Unilateral Nuclear Disarmament." Philosophy and Public Affairs 12 (Summer 1983).

Roberts, Chalmers. The Nuclear Years. Westport, CT: Praeger, 1970.

Rostow, Eugene V. "The Case Against SALT II." Commentary, June 1979, pp. 25-32.

Rowen, Henry S. "Objectives and Dysfunctions of Arms Negotiations: The Salt Experience." In: Soviet Power and Western Negotiating Policies, vol. 2: The Western

<u>Panacea: Constraining Soviet Power Through Negotiations</u>, pp. 55-65. Edited by Uwe Nerlich. Cambridge, MA: Ballinger, 1984.

Schear, James A. "Arms Control Treaty Compliance: Buildup to a Breakdown?" <u>International Security</u> 9 (Fall 1985): 141-82.

Schear, James A. "Verifying Arms Agreements: Premises, Practices, and Future Problems." <u>Arms Control</u> (December 1982): 76-95.

Schell, Jonathan. "Credibility." Part VI of "The Time of Illusion." <u>New Yorker</u>, July 7, 1975, pp. 30-48.

Schelling, Thomas C. "A Framework for the Evaluation of Arms Control Proposals." <u>Daedelus</u> 104 (Summer 1975): 187-200.

Schelling, Thomas C. "The Future of Arms Control." <u>Operations Research</u> (September-October 1961): 722-31.

Schelling, Thomas, and Morton Halperin. <u>Strategy and Arms Control</u>. New York: The Twentieth Century Fund, 1961. (3)

Scribner, R., T. Ralston, and W. Metz. <u>The Verification Challenge: Problems and Promise of Strategic Arms Control</u>. Boston: Birkhauser, 1985.

Sharp, Jane M.O. "Restructuring the Arms Control Dialogue." <u>International Security</u> 6 (Winter 1981-82): 144-76.

Sienkiewicz, Stanley. "SALT and Soviet Nuclear Doctrine." <u>International Security</u> 2 (Spring 1978).

Sigal, Leon V. "Warming to the Freeze," <u>Foreign Policy</u> (Fall, 1982): 54-65.

Slocombe, Walter B. <u>Technology and the Future of Arms Control</u>. Adelphi Paper 198. London: International Institute for Strategic Studies, 1984, pp. 39-47.

Slocombe, Walter B. "Verification and Negotiation." In: <u>The Nuclear Freeze and Arms Control</u>. Edited by Miller. Cambridge, MA: Ballinger, 1984.

Bibliography

Smith, Gerard. <u>Doubletalk: The Story of SALT I</u>. New York: Doubleday, 1980. (2)

"Special SALT Issue." <u>Arms Control Today</u> 9 (July/August 1979): 16pp.

Stuckel, Donald J. <u>Technology and Arms Control</u>. Washington, DC: Government Printing Office, 1978.

Sykes and Evenden. "Verification of a Comprehensive Test Ban." <u>Scientific American</u>, October, 1982.

"Symposium: Is Arms Control Obsolete?" <u>Harper's</u>. July 1985. pp. 35-41.

Talbot, David. "And Now They are Doves." <u>Mother Jones</u>, May 1984, pp. 26-33, 47-50, 60.

Talbott, Strobe. "Arms Control: Making the Wrong Moves?" <u>Time</u>, April 18, 1983, pp. 16-29.

Talbott, Strobe. "Battling the Gods of War." <u>Time</u>, June 25. 1984, pp. 30-44. (2)

Talbott, Strobe. "Buildup and Breakdown." <u>Foreign Affairs</u> 62 (1983): 587-615.

Thompson, E.P., and D. Smith, eds. <u>Protest and Survive</u>. New York: Monthly Review Press, 1981.

Thorrson, Inga. "Disarmament and Global Security: Interview on the UN Special Session." <u>Alternatives: A Journal of World Policy</u> 8 (1982): 247-57.

US Arms Control and Disarmament Agency. <u>Arms Control and Disarmament Agreements</u>. Washington DC: Government Printing Office, 1982.

US Congress. House. Armed Services Committee. <u>Statement of Hans A. Bethe at Hearings before a subcommittee of the House Armed Services Committee on H.R. 3073, The People Protection Act</u>. 98th Cong., 1st sess. Washington, DC: Government Printing Office, 1983.

US Congress. Senate. Committee on Foreign Relations. <u>The SALT II Treaty: Hearings before the Committee on Foreign Relations</u>, 96th Congress., 1st sess. Washington, DC: Government Printing Office, 1979.

US Congress. Senate. Select Committee on Intelligence. Capabilities of the United States to Monitor the SALT II Treaty. 96th Cong., 1st sess. Washington, DC: Government Printing Office, 1979.

US Department of Defense. Compliance and Verification in SALT. Selected Document No. 7. Washington, DC: Government Printing Office, 1978. 14 pp.

US Department of State. Salt II Agreement. Selected Document No. 12B. Washington, DC: Government Printing Office, 1979.

US Department of State. SALT II Testimony. Bureau of Public Affairs. Current Policy No. 72A. Washington, DC: Government Printing Office, 1979.

US Executive Office of the President. The President's Unclassified Report to the Congress on Soviet Noncompliance with Arms Control Agreements. February 1, 1985.

Wohlstetter, Albert. "Is There a Strategic Arms Race?" Foreign Policy 15 (Summer 1974): 3-20.

Wohlstetter, Albert. "Rivals, But No Race." Foreign Policy 16 (Fall 1974): 49-81.

Wolfe, John. The SALT Experience. Cambridge: Ballinger, 1979.

York, Herbert R. "Arms Limitations Strategies." Physics Today, March 1983, pp. 24-30.

York, Herbert R., and G. Allen Greb. "The Comprehensive Test Ban." In: Science and Ethical Responsibility, pp. 124-42. Edited by Sanford Lakoff, Jeffrey Leifer, Ronald Bee and Eric Markusen. Boston: Addison-Wesley, 1980.

NUCLEAR PROLIFERATION:

This section includes discussions of reasons and methods for preventing or slowing the spread of nuclear weapons technology to persons or governments who have not previously acquired it, with reference to nuclear reactor sales and exports, thefts of nuclear materials, international nonproliferation agreements and organizations.

Bibliography

Alm, Alvin L. "Energy Supply Interruptions and National Security." <u>Science</u>, March 27, 1981, pp. 1379-85.

Brenner, Michael. "Carter's Bungled Promises." <u>Foreign Policy</u> 36 (Fall 1979): 89-100.

Cochran, Thomas B. "Secrecy and Nuclear Power." <u>Bulletin of Atomic Scientists</u> 37 (Aug./Sept. 1981): 37-41.

Dowty, Alan. "Nuclear Proliferation: The Israeli Case." <u>International Studies Quarterly</u> 22 (March 1978): 79-120.

Epstein, William. "The Proliferation of Nuclear Weapons." <u>Scientific American</u>, April 1975, pp. 18-33.

Greenwood, Ted, George Rathgens, and Jack Ruina. <u>Nuclear Power and Weapons Proliferation</u>. Adelphi Paper 130. London: International Institute for Strategic Studies, 1979. (2)

Jenkins, Brian Michael, et al. "Nuclear Terrorism and Its Consequences." <u>Society</u>, July/August 1980, pp. 5-25.

Jones, Rodney K.,ed. <u>Small Nuclear Forces and US Security Policy</u>. Lexington, MA: Lexington Books, 1984. pp. 243-256, 155-181.

Kennan, George. "International Control of Atomic Energy." <u>Foreign Relations of the United States, 1950</u> 1 (1950): 22-44.

Lawrence, Robert M., and Joel Larus. <u>Nuclear Proliferation: Phase II</u>. Lawrence, KS: University Press of Kansas, 1974.

Lifton, Robert Jay, and Robert Falk. <u>Indefensible Weapons: The Political and Psychological Case Against Nuclearism</u>. New York: Basic Books, 1982. (2)

Lovins, Amory, and Hunter Lovins. <u>Energy/War: Breaking the Nuclear Link</u>. San Francisco: Friends of the Earth, 1981.

McPhee, John. <u>The Curve of Binding Energy</u>. New York: Ballantine, 1975.

Norman, Colin. "Weapons Builders Eye Civilian Nuclear Fuel." Science, Oct. 16, 1981, pp. 307-08.

Nye, Joseph. "Non-Proliferation: A Long-Term Strategy." Foreign Affairs 56 (April 1978): 601-23.

Nye, Joseph. "We Tried Harder (and Did More)." Foreign Policy 44 (Fall 1979): 101-94.

Physicians for Social Responsibility. Preparing for Nuclear War: the Psychological Effects. New York: Physicians for Social Responsibility, 1982.

Rose and Lester. "Nuclear Power, Nuclear Weapons and International Stability". Scientific American, April, 1978, pp. 45-57.

Salaff, Stephen. "The Plutonium Connection: Energy and Arms." Bulletin of Atomic Scientists 36 (Sept. 1980): 18-23.

Spector, Leonard S. The New Nuclear Nations. New York: Vintage Books, 1985. (2)

Spector, Leonard S. Nuclear Proliferation Today. New York: Vintage, 1984.

US Congress. Senate. Committee on Foreign Relations. Prospects for Multilateral Arms Export Restraint. 96th Cong, 1st sess. Washington, DC: Government Printing Office, 1979.

Waltz, Kenneth. The Spread of Nuclear Weapons: More May be Better. Adelphi Paper 171. London: International Institute for Strategic Studies, 1981.

EUROPEAN SECURITY:

This section includes discussions of cultural, historical, economic, political and strategic dimensions of European security, with reference to alliances and both nuclear and nonnuclear forces.

Agnew, Harold M. "A Primer on Enhanced Radiation Weapons." Bulletin of Atomic Scientists 33 (December 1977): 6-8.

Bibliography

Bertram, Christopher. "The Implications of Theater Nuclear Weapons in Europe." Foreign Affairs 60 (1981-82): 305-26. (2)

Black, Edwin F., and S. T. Cohen. "The Neutron Bomb and the Defense of NATO." Military Review, May 1978, pp. 53-61.

Bundy, McGeorge. "America in the 1980's: Reframing our Relations with our Friends and Among our Allies." Survival 24 (January-February 1982): 24-31.

Bundy, McGeorge, George F. Kennan, Robert S. McNamara, and Gerard Smith. "Nuclear Weapons and the Atlantic Alliance." Foreign Affairs 60 (1982): 753-68. (5)

Canby, Steven. "NATO Muscle: More Shadow Than Substance." Foreign Policy 8 (Fall 1972): 38-49.

Coit, Dennis Blacker, and Farooq Hussain. "European Theater Nuclear Forces." Bulletin of Atomic Scientists 36 (October 1980): 32-37. (2)

Cordesman, Anthony. Deterrence in the 1980's: Part I. Adelphi Paper 165. London: International Institute for Strategic Studies. 1981.

De Rose, Francois. "Updating Deterrence in Europe: Inflexible Response?" Survival 24 (January-February 1984).

Donnelly, Chris. "The Soviet Operational Maneuver Group." International Defense Review 15 (1982): 1177-86.

Doty, P., and G. Treverton. "Whither the Nuclear Confrontation?" In: The Nuclear Confrontation in Europe. Edited by J. Boutwell, P. Doty, and G. Treverton. London: Croom Helm, 1985.

Flanagan, S., and F. Hampson. Securing Europe's Future: Changing Elements of European Security. London: Croom Helm, 1986. pp. 302-18.

Franck, Thomas M. "The President, the Constitution and Nuclear Weapons." In: Nuclear Weapons and Law, edited by A. Miller and M. Feinrider, pp. 363-68. Westport, CT: Greenwood Press, 1984.

Freedman, Lawrence. "A Critique of the END Campaign." Bulletin of Atomic Scientists 37 (December 1981): 38-42.

Garthoff, Raymond L. "Brezhnev's Opening: The TNF Tangle." Foreign Policy 41 (Winter 1980-81): 82-94. (2)

Helprin, Mark. "Drawing the Line in Europe: The Case for Missile Deployment." New York Times Magazine, December 4, 1983. pp. 53-54, 56, 104-107.

Herf, Jeffrey. "War, Peace, and the Intellectuals: The West German Peace Movement." International Security 10 (Spring 1986): 172-200.

Holdren, John P. "Extended Deterrence, No-First-Use, and European Security," pp. 191-202. In: Nuclear Weapons and Europe. Edited by Paolo C. Ramusino and Francesco Lenci. Milan: Scientia-U.S.P.I.D., 1986.

International Institute for Strategic Studies. The Military Balance, 1982-1983. London: International Institute for Strategic Studies, 1982. pp. 129-136.

Kaldor, Mary. "END Can be a Beginning." Bulletin of Atomic Scientists 37 (December 1981): 42-64.

Kemp, Geoffrey. Nuclear for Medium Forces. Adelphi Papers 106 & 107. London: International Institute for Strategic Studies, 1974.

Kissinger, Henry A. "NATO: The Next Thirty Years." Survival 21 (1979).

Komer, Robert. "Is Conventional Defense of Europe Feasible?" Naval War College Review 35 (1982): 80-91.

Luttwak, Edward. "The American Style of Warfare and the Military Balance." Survival 21 (1979): 57-69.

Mearsheimer, John J. "Maneuver Mobile Defense and NATO Central Front." International Security 7 (1981/82): 104-122.

Mearsheimer, John J. "Nuclear Weapons and Deterrence in Europe." International Security 9 (Winter 1984/85): 19-46.

Bibliography

Mearsheimer, John J. "Why The Soviets Can't Win Quickly in Central Europe." <u>International Security</u> 7 (1982): 3-39. (3)

Merritt, Jack N., and Pierre M. Sprey. "Negative Marginal Returns in Weapons Acquisition." In: <u>American Defense Policy</u>, 3d ed, pp. 486-95. Edited by Richard G. Head and Ervin J. Rokke. Baltimore: Johns Hopkins, 1973.

Miller, A., and M. Feinrider, eds. <u>Nuclear Weapons and Law</u>. Westport CT: Greenwood Press, 1984.

Paine, Christopher. "Pershing II: The Army's Strategic Weapon." <u>Bulletin of Atomic Scientists</u> 36 (October 1980): 25-31.

Posen, Barry R. "Inadvertent Nuclear War? Escalation and NATO's Northern Flank." <u>International Security</u> 7 (1982): 28-54. (4)

Posen, Barry R. "Measuring the European Conventional Balance." <u>International Security</u> 9 (1984-85): 47-88.

Record, Jeffrey. "Should America Pay for Europe's Security?" <u>Washington Quarterly</u> 5 (Winter 1982): 19-23.

Record, Jeffrey, "Theater Nuclear Weapons: Begging the Soviet Union to Preempt." <u>Survival</u> 19 (September-October 1977): 208-11.

Ruhle, Hans. "Cruise Missiles, NATO and the 'European Option'." <u>Strategic Review</u> 6 (1978): 46-52.

Schmidt, Helmut. "The 1977 Alastair Budhan Memorial Lecture." <u>Survival</u> 20 (1978): 2-10.

Sherr, Alan B. "The European Nuclear Negotiations: Paths to War or Peace?" Boston: Lawyers Alliance for Nuclear Arms Control, 1983.

Sherwin, Martin. <u>A World Destroyed: The Atomic Bomb and the Grand Alliance</u>. New York: Alfred Knopf, 1975. (3)

Smith, Dan. "The European Nuclear Theatre." In: <u>Protest and Survive</u>, pp. 55-69. Edited by E.P. Thompson and Dan Smith. New York: Monthly Review Press, 1981.

Solomon, Norman. "Letter to E.P. Thompson: Europe, Russia, and the US Missiles." The Nation, April 16, 1983, pp. 469-72.

Soviet Committee for European Security and Cooperation. The Threat to Europe. Moscow: Progress Publishers, 1981.

Stone, Jeremy. "Presidential First Use Is Unlawful." Foreign Policy 56 (Fall 1984): 94-102.

Swee, William. "Europe's Peace Movement: Topic or Target?" Columbia Journalism Review (September/October 1983): 46-50.

Thompson, E.P. "END and the Soviet 'Peace Offensive.'" The Nation, February 26, 1983.

Thompson, E.P. "Replay from Europe: Peace is a Third-Way Street." The Nation, April 16, 1983, pp. 472-3, 476-81.

Treverton, Gregory. Nuclear Weapons in Europe. Adelphi Paper 168. London: International Institute for Strategic Studies, 1981.

US Congress. Congressional Budget Office. Planning US General Purpose Forces: The Theatre Nuclear Forces. Washington, DC: Government Printing Office, 1977. 45 pp.

Winkler, Theodor. Arms Control and the Politics of European Security. Adelphi Paper 177. London: International Institute for Strategic Studies, 1982.

INTERVENTION IN FOREIGN STATES:

This section includes discussion of actual or proposed armed interventions in one state by another, including Korea, Vietnam, and Central America.

Berryman, Phillip. What's Wrong in Central America and What to do About It. Philadelphia: American Friends Service Committee, 1983.

Center for Defense Information. "A World at War: Small Wars and Superpower Military Intervention." Defense Monitor 8 (1979).

Bibliography

Dinerstein, Herbert S. *Intervention Against Communism*.
Baltimore: Johns Hopkins Press, 1967. 52 pp.

Ellsberg, Daniel. *Papers on the War*. New York: Simon
& Schuster, 1972.

Forsberg, Randall. "The Case for a Nonintervention Re-
gime." *Defense & Disarmament News* 3 (August/September
1987): 3pp.

Schaefer, Michael. "Mineral Myths." *Foreign Policy*
47 (1982): 154-71.

Shawcross, William. *Sideshow: Kissinger, Nixon, and
the Destruction of Cambodia*. New York: Simon and
Schuster, 1981. Pp. 19-35, 280-299.

Sheehan, N. *The Pentagon Papers*. New York: Bantam
Books, 1971.

HISTORY OF NUCLEAR WEAPONS DEVELOPMENT:

This section includes discussion of the historical
development of nuclear weapons and their use at Hiroshima and Nagasaki, with reference to persons involved,
their motives, and second-thoughts.

Anders, Gunther. "Reflections on the H-Bomb." In:
Voices of Dissent, pp. 359-68. Edited by Irving Howe.
New York: Grove Press, 1958.

Baker, Paul R., ed. *The Atomic Bomb: The Great Decision*, 2d. Hinsdale, IL: Dryden Press, 1976.

Bernstein, Barton J. "The Dropping of the A-Bomb."
Center Magazine (March/April 1983): 7-15.

Bernstein, Barton J. "Truman and the H-Bomb." *Bulletin
of Atomic Scientists* 40 (March 1984): 12-18.

Bethe, Hans A. "Comments on the History of the
H-Bomb." *Los Alamos Science*, Fall 1982, pp. 43-53.

Carey, Michael. "The Schools and Civil Defense: The
Fifties Revisited." *Teachers College Record* 84 (1982):
115-127.

Donovan, Robert J. *Eisenhower: The Inside Story.* New
York: Harper, 1956. pp. 114-25.

Einstein, Albert, and Bertrand Russell. "The Einstein-Russell Manifesto." In: <u>Scientists in Quest for Peace: A History of the Pugwash Conferences</u>. Edited by Joseph Rotblat. Cambridge: M.I.T. Press, 1972.

Eubank, Keith, ed. <u>The Road to World War II: A Documentary History</u>. Arlington Heights, IL: Harlan Davidson, 1973, pp. 71-106, 135-43, 203-19.

Feis, Herbert. <u>The Atomic Bomb and the End of WW II</u>. Princeton: Princeton University Press, 1966. pp. 119-146.

Feld, Bernard T. "Einstein and the Politics of Nuclear Weapons." <u>Bulletin of Atomic Scientists</u> 35 (March 1979): 5-16.

Franck, James, et al. "The Franck Report: June 11, 1945." In: <u>A Peril and A Hope: The Scientists' Movement in America 1945-47</u>, pp. 371-83. Edited by Alice Kimball Smith. Cambridge, MA: M.I.T. Press, 1970.

Fussell, Paul. <u>The Great War and Modern Memory</u>. New York: Oxford University Press, 1977.

Fussell, Paul. "Hiroshima: A Soldiers's View," <u>The New Republic</u>, August 22, 1981, pp. 26-30. (2)

Fussell, Paul, and Michael Walzer. "An Exchange on Hiroshima," <u>The New Republic</u>, September 23, 1981, pp. 13-14. (2)

Gerber, Larry. "The Baruch Plan and the Origins of the Cold War." <u>Diplomatic History</u> 6 (Winter 1982): 69-95.

Herkin, Gregg. "'A Most Deadly Illusion': The Atomic Secret and Nuclear Weapons Policy, 1945-1950." <u>Pacific Historical Review</u> 49 (February 1980): 51-76.

Hersey, John. <u>Hiroshima</u>. New York: Bantam Books, 1959. (6)

Iwamatsu, Shigetoshi. "A Perspective on the War Crimes." <u>Bulletin of Atomic Scientists</u> (February 1982): 29-32.

Jungk, Robert. <u>Brighter Than a Thousand Suns: A Personal History of the Atomic Scientists</u>. Translated by

Bibliography

James Cleugh. San Diego: Harcourt, Brace, Jovanovich, 1970. (4)

Kaplan, Fred. *The Wizards of Armageddon*. Beaverton, OR: Touchstone Press, 1984.

Kennan, George. *American Diplomacy, 1900-1950*. Chicago: University of Chicago Press, 1985.

Kissinger, Henry. *The White House Years*. New York: Little and Brown, 1979.

Lessing, Doris. *Memoirs of a Survivor*. New York: Knopf, 1975.

Lyon, Peter. *Eisenhower: Portrait of a Hero.* Boston: Little and Brown, 1974. Pp. 534-36.

Melanson, Philip H. "Atomic Bomb Test Secrets: The Human Guinea Pigs at Bikini." *The Nation*, July 9, 1983, pp. 33, 48-50.

Quester, George. *Nuclear Diplomacy: The First Twenty-Five Years*. N. p.: Dunellen Co., 1970.

Rosenburg, David. "The Origins of Overkill: Nuclear Weapons and American Strategy, 1945-1960." *International Security* 7 (1983): 3-71. (2)

Schilling, Warner. "The H-Bomb Decision: How to Decide Without Really Choosing." *Political Science Quarterly* 76 (1961): 24-46.

Schwartz, Richard Alan. "What the File Tells: The FBI and Dr. Einstein." *The Nation*, September 3, 1983, pp. 168-73.

Shepley, James. "How Dulles Averted War." *Life Magazine*, January 16, 1966, pp. 70-80.

Sherwin, Martin. "The New A-Bomb Debate: Hiroshima and Modern Memory," *The Nation*, October 10, 1981, pp. 329, 349-353. (2)

Smith, Alice Kimball. "Manhattan Project: The Atomic Bomb." In: *The Nuclear Almanac*, pp. 21-43. Edited by Jack Dennis. Reading MA: Addison-Wesley, 1984.

Smith, Alice Kimball, and Charles Weiner, eds. Robert Oppenheimer: Letters and Recollections. Cambridge, MA: Harvard University Press, 1980.

Stern, Philip. The Oppenheimer Case: Security on Trial. New York: Harper and Row, 1969, pp. 480-504.

Szulc, Tad. "The Untold Story of How Russia Got the Bomb." Los Angeles Times, August 26, 1984, Part IV, p. 1.

Thurlow, Setsuko. "Nuclear War in Human Perspective: A Survivor's Report." American Journal of Orthopsychiatry 52 (1982): 638-45.

Titus, James, ed. The Home Front and War in the Twentieth Century: The American Experience in Comparative Perspective. Proceedings of the USAF Military Academy Military History Symposium Series. Washington, DC: Office of Air Force History, 1983. pp. 5-17, 47-56, 91-110.

US National Security Council. "The Position of the United States with Respect to Soviet-Directed World Communism." NSC 7, Washington, DC, March 30, 1948. 10pp.

Weisgall, Jonathan. "The Nuclear Nomads of Bikini." Foreign Policy 39 (Summer 1980): 74-98.

Whitner, Lawrence S. Rebels Against War: The American Peace Movement, 1941-1960. New York: Columbia University Press, 1969. chap. 5.

Wigutoff, Sharon, and Sergui Herscovivi. "The Treatment of Militarism in History Textbooks." Education Digest (March 1983).

York, Herbert, and C. Allen Greb. "The Superbomb." In: The Nuclear Almanac, pp. 53-65. Edited by Jack Dennis. Reading, MA: Addison Wesley, 1984.

Young, Louise B. The Mystery of Matter. New York: Oxford University Press, 1965.

CULTURAL CONTEXT:

This section includes discussions of political culture and socialization since nuclear weapons were

Bibliography

developed and used, with treatment of how the news media covers nuclear arms.

American Friends Service Committee. _Makers of the Nuclear Holocaust_. Philadelphia: American Friends Service Committee, 1981.

Basnow, E. _The Evolution of American Television_. New York: Oxford Press, 1975.

Bender, David L., and Brune Leone. _War and Human Nature_. St. Paul: Greenhaven Press, 1983. Pp. 147-72.

Booth, Ken. "American Strategy: The Myths Revisited." In: _American Thinking About Peace and War_, pp. 1-35. Edited by Ken Booth and Moorhead Wright. New York: Harper & Row, 1978.

Brown, Robert McAfee. "The Debasement of Language." _The Christian Century_, April 6, 1983, pp. 313-315.

Burt, Richard, et al. "Covering Arms Control: A TWQ Roundtable." _Washington Quarterly_ 5 (Fall 1982): 143-150.

Broyles, William, Jr. "Why Men Love War." _Esquire_, November, 1984, pp. 55-65.

Cockburn, Alexander. "Graphic Evidence of Nuclear Confusion." _Columbia Journalism Review_ 22 (May/June 1983): 38-41.

Cohn, Carol. "Nuclear Language and How We Learned to Pat the Bomb." _Bulletin of Atomic Scientists_ (June 1987): 17-24.

Delauer, Richard D. "Shape Up! A Pentagon View of the Press." _Columbia Journalism Review_ 22 (September/October 1983): 46-50.

DeRivera, J. _The Psychological Dimension of Foreign Policy_. Columbus, OH: Merrill Publishing, 1968. Chapter 19.

Drell, Sidney. "Newspeak and Nukespeak." In: _On 1984_. Edited by Peter Stansky. New York: W.H. Freeman, 1983.

Nuclear Weapons in the University Classroom

Galey, Margaret. "The Nairobi Conference: The Power-
less Majority." PS 19 (Spring 1986): 255-65.

Gerzon, Mark. A Choice of Heroes: The Changing Face
of American Manhood. Boston: Houghton Mifflin, 1982.

Gray, Colin. Nuclear Strategy and National Style.
Lanham, MD: Hamilton Press, 1986.

Hampshire, S. Morality and Pessimism. New York: Cambridge University Press, 1972.

Joseph, Gloria. "The Incompatible Menage a Trois:
Marxism, Feminism, and Racism." In: Women and Revolu-
tion, pp. 91-108. Edited by Lydia Sargent. Boston:
South End Press, 1981.

Manoff, Robert Karl. "The Media: Nuclear Secrecy vs
Democracy." Bulletin of Atomic Scientists (1984):
26-29.

Morris, Roger. "Reporting for Duty: The Pentagon and
the Press." Columbia Journalism Review (Septem-
ber/October 1983): 17-20.

Musil, Robert K. "On Calling a Bomb a Bomb." Nuclear
Times, March 1983, pp. 26-28.

Rapoport, Anatol. Fights, Games and Debates. Ann Arbor, MI: University of Michigan Press, 1974.

Reardon, Betty. "A Gender Analysis of Militarism and
Sexist Repression: A Suggested Research Agenda." International Peace Research News Letter 21 (1983):
3-10.

Ruether, Rosemary Radford. "Feminism and Peace." The
Christian Century, August 31, 1983. pp. 771-776.

Shulstad, Raymond A. Peace is My Profession: A Sol-
dier's View of the Moral Dimension of US Nuclear Policy. Washington, DC: National Defense University,
1986.

Smith, Barbara. "Fractious, Kicking, Messy, Free:
Feminist Writers Confront the Nuclear Abyss." New England Review/Bread Loaf Quarterly 5 (Summer 1983):
581-582.

Bibliography

Spretnak, Charlene. "Naming the Cultural Forces that Push Us Toward War." Journal of Humanistic Psychology 25 (Summer 1983): 104-114.

Wilson, Ward. "Nuclear Ignorance." Bulletin of Atomic Scientists 37 (1981): 24-25.

ARMS RACE:

This section includes discussion of the history, causes, economics and politics of weapons acquisitions, defense spending, force development and strategic modernization, with reference to the role of the "military-industrial complex."

Abel, Ellie. The Missile Crisis. Philadelphia: Lippincott, 1966.

Adams, Gordon, and David Gold. "Recasting the Military Spending Debate." Bulletin of Atomic Scientists (October 1986): 26-32.

Adams, R., and S. Cullen, eds. The Final Epidemic. Chicago: University of Chicago Press, 1982.

Allison, Graham T. "Questions About the Arms Race: Who's Racing Whom? A Bureaucratic Perspective." In: Contrasting Approaches to Strategic Arms Control, pp. 31-72. Edited by Robert L. Pfaltzgraff. Lexington MA: Lexington Books, 1974.

Allison, Graham T., and Frederic A. Morris. "Armaments and Arms Control: Exploring the Determinants of Military Weapons." Daedalus (Summer 1975): 99-129.

Anderson, J. Edward. "First Strike: Myth or Reality." Bulletin of Atomic Scientists 37 (November 1981): 6-11.

Anderson, Marion. The Impact of Military Spending on the Machinists Union. Washington, DC: International Association of Machinists, 1979.

Aspin, Les. "Judge Not by Numbers Alone." Bulletin of Atomic Scientists 36 (June 1980): 28-33. (3)

Ball, Desmond. Politics and Force Levels: The Strategic Missile Program of the Kennedy Administration. Berkeley: University of California Press, 1980.

117

Barnaby, Frank, and Ronald Huisken. Arms Uncontrolled. Cambridge, MA: Harvard University Press, 1971.

Bennett. "Arms Transfer as an Instrument of Soviet Policy in the Middle East." Middle East Journal (Autumn 1985): 745-74.

Berghahn, V.R. Germany and the Approach of the War in 1914. New York: St. Martins, 1973, pp. 104-24 and 211-14.

Berman, Robert, and John Baker. Soviet Strategic Forces. Washington, DC: Brookings Institution, 1983.

Boston Study Group. The Price of Defense. New York: New York Times Book Company, 1979.

Broad, William J. "Military Grapples with the Chaos Factor." Science, September 11, 1981, pp. 1228-29.

Buchan, Glenn C. "The Anti-MAD Mythology." Bulletin of Atomic Scientists 37 (April 1981): 13-17.

Carnesale, Albert, and Charles Glaser. "ICBM Vulnerability: The Cures are Worse than the Disease." International Security 7 (1982): 70-85. (2)

Center for Defense Information. "US Nuclear Weapons Accidents: Danger in our Midst." Defense Monitor 11 (1981).

Chivian, E., S. Chivian, R. J. Lifton, and J. E. Mack, eds. Last Aid. San Francisco: W. H. Freeman, 1982.

Craig, Paul, and John Jungerman. The Nuclear Arms Race: Technology and Society. New York: McGraw Hill, 1986.

Coulam, Robert F. "The Inter-Service Weapons Rivalry." Bulletin of Atomic Scientists 33 (June 1977): 25-35.

Day, Samuel H., Jr. "The Nicest People Make the Bomb." In: Time Bomb: A Nuclear Reader from the Progressive, pp. 56-61. Edited by James Rowen. Madison, WI: Progressive Foundation, 1980.

DeGrasse, Robert, Jr., and Paul Murphy. "The High Cost of Rearmament." Bulletin of Atomic Scientists 37 (October 1981): 16-23.

Bibliography

Downs, George, David Rocke, and Randolph Siverson. "Arms Races and Cooperation." World Politics 38 (October 1985). (2)

Drell, Sidney, and Eric Von Hippel. "Limited Nuclear War." Scientific American, November 1976, pp. 27-37. (3)

Drell, Sidney D. "SUM." Arms Control Today 9 (September 1979): 1-8.

Dumas, Llyod J. "Human Fallibility and Weapons." Bulletin of Atomic Scientists 36 (November 1980): 15-19.

Eisenhower, Dwight D. "Liberty is at Stake." Vital Speeches 28 (1961): 228-31.

Ellsberg, Daniel. "Call to Mutiny." In: Protest and Survive, pp. i-xxxviii. Edited by E.P. Thompson and Dan Smith. New York: Monthly Review Press, 1981.

Enthoven, Alain C., and K. Wayne Smith. How Much Is Enough? Shaping the Defense Program, 1961-69. New York: Harper & Row, 1971. Pp. 117-84. (3)

Farmazyan, R. Disarmament and the Economy. Chicago: Imported Publications, 1981. pp. 45-73.

Ford, Daniel. "A Reporter at Large: The Button." New Yorker, April 1, 1985, pp. 43-91 and April 8, 1985, pp. 49-92.

Freedman, Lawrence. "Nuclear Weapons in Europe: Is There an Arms Race?" Millenium (Spring 1984): 57-64.

Galbraith, John Kenneth. "The Economics of the Arms Race--and After." Bulletin of Atomic Scientists 37a (June/July 1981): 13-16.

Gansler, Jacques. "Can the Defense Industry Respond to the Reagan Initiatives?" International Security 6 (1982): 102-121.

Gansler, Jacques. "We Can Afford Security." Foreign Policy 51 (Summer 1983): 64-83. (2)

Gansler, J., and S. Melman. "The Military Industrial Complex: A Debate." Defense Management Journal 15 (1979): 1-13.

Goldman, Ralph. "Political Distrust as Generator of the Arms Race: Prisoners and Security Dilemmas." In: Toward Nuclear Disarmament and Global Security, pp. 90-94. Edited by Burns H. Weston. Boulder, CO: Westview Press, 1984.

Gore, Albert, Jr. "The Fork in the Road: A New Plan for Nuclear Peace." New Republic, May 5, 1982, pp. 13-16.

Gray, Colin S. "The Arms Race Phenomenon." World Politics 24 (January 1972): 39-79.

Gray, Colin S. "The Urge to Compete: Rationales for Arms Racing." World Politics 26 (1974): 207-233.

Greb, G. A., and G. W. Johnson. "A History of Strategic Arms Limitation." Bulletin of Atomic Scientists 40 (1984): 30-37.

Greenwood, Ted. "Conclusion." In: Making the MIRV, pp. 150-172. Cambridge, MA: Ballantine Books, 1975.

Halperin, Morton H., et al. Bureaucratic Politics and Foreign Policy. Washington, DC: Brookings, 1972. Pp. 26-62; Chap. 3. (2)

Halperin, Morton, et al. "Organizational Interests." In: American Defense Policy, pp. 207-223. Edited by John E. Endicott and Roy W. Stafford. Baltimore: Johns Hopkins, 1977.

Hewlett, Richard, and Oscar Anderson. The New World. Pennsylvania University Press, 1962. Chaps. 15 and 16.

Hitch, Charles. The Economics of Defense in the Nuclear Age. New York: Atheneum, 1965.

Holdren, Johm P. "The Dynamics of the Nuclear Arms Race: History, Status, Prospects." In: Nuclear Weapons and the Future of Humanity: The Fundamental Questions, pp. 41-83. Edited by A. Cohen and S. Lee. Totowa, NJ: Rowman & Allenheld, 1986.

Holtzman, Franklyn. "Are The Soviets Really Outspending the U.S. on Defense?" International Security 5 (1980): 86-104.

Bibliography

Holtzman, Franklyn. "Are We Falling Behind the Soviets?" Atlantic, July, 1983, pp. 10-18.

Huntington, Samuel. "Arms Races: Prerequisites and Results." Public Policy (1958): 41-86. (3)

Kaplan, Fred. Dubious Spector: A Skeptical Look at the Soviet Nuclear Threat. Washington, DC: Institute of Policy Studies, 1984.

Kaufmann, William W. The 1986 Defense Budget. Washington, DC: Brookings, 1985. pp. 7-23.

Kaufmann, William W. A Reasonable Defense. Washington, DC: Brookings, 1986.

Kennedy, Paul. "Arms Races and the Causes of War." In: Strategy and Diplomacy 1870-1945. Winchester, MA: Allen and Unwin, 1984. pp. 163-179.

Kincade, William H. "The View from the Pentagon." Arms Control Today 7 (1977): 1-4.

Kistiakowsky, George B. "False Alarm Over SALT." New York Review of Books, March 22, 1979, pp. 33-38.

Klare, Michael. "Making Nuclear War Thinkable." The Nation, April 13, 1974, pp. 461-66.

Kurth, James. "Why We Buy the Weapons We Do." Foreign Policy 11 (Summer 1973): 33-56.

Lafeber, Walter. "Foreign Policy Assumptions of the Reagan Military Budget." In: Defense Sense: The Search for a Rational Military Policy. Edited by Patrick O. Heffernan. Cambridge, MA: Ballinger, 1983.

Lambelet, John C. "The Anglo-German Dreadnought Race 1905-1914." The Papers of the Peace Science Society (International) 22 (1974).

Leontief, W., and F. Duchin. Military Spending: Facts and Figures, World-wide Implications and Future Outlook. New York: Oxford University Press, 1983.

Lewis, Thomas. Lives of a Cell: Notes of a Biology Walker. New York: Viking, 1974. pp. 29-30, 103-110.

McBride, Steward. "New Life for Nuclear City." New York Times Magazine, January 18, 1981, pp. 28-36.

Morrison, Phillip, and Paul F. Walker. "A New Strategy for Military Spending." Scientific American, October 1978: 48-61. (2)

Mumford, Lewis. "The Morals of Extermination." In: No Place to Hide, pp. 193-205. Edited by Seymor Melman. New York: Grove Press, 1962.

Nash, Henry T. "The Bureaucratization of Homocide." Bulletin of Atomic Scientists 36 (April 1980): 22-27.

Nitze, Paul H. "Deterring our Deterrent." Foreign Policy 25 (Winter 1976-77): 195-210.

Pechman, Joseph A. Setting National Priorities: Agenda for the 1980s. Washington, DC: Brookings, 1980. pp. 59-99.

Pierre, Andrew. "Arms Sales: The New Diplomacy." Foreign Affairs (Winter 1981-82): 266-86.

Pike, John E. "Corporate Interest in SDI." F.A.S. Public Interest Report 40 (April 1987): 1-10.

Pipes, Richard. US-Soviet Relations in the Era of Detente. Boulder, CO: Westview Press, 1981.

Rathjens, George. "The Dynamics of the Arms Race." Scientific American, April 1969, pp. 15-25.

Ravenal, Earl C. "Cutting the Defense Budget." In: Defense Sense: The Search for a Rational Military Policy. Edited by Patrick O'Heffernan. Cambridge, MA: Ballinger, 1983.

Rowen, Henry. "The Need for a New Analytical Framework." International Security 1 (1976): 130-46.

Russett, Bruce. "What's Wrong with Arms Races?" and "Why do Arms Races Occur?' In: The Prisoners of Insecurity: Nuclear Deterrance, The Arms Race, and Arms Control, pp. 47-66, 69-96. San Francisco: W.H. Freeman, 1983.

Schwartz, Charles. "The Corporate Connection." Bulletin of Atomic Scientists (October 1975): 15-19.

Bibliography

Scott, Harriet, and William Scott. <u>The Armed Forces and the USSR</u>. Boulder, CO: Westview Press, 1979.

Sherman, Stafford P. "How Rockwell Kept the B-1 Alive." <u>Fortune</u>, April 1980, pp. 22-27.

Sklar, H., ed. <u>Trilateralism</u>. Boston: South End Press, 1980.

Steiner, Zara S. <u>Britain and the Origins of the First World War</u>. New York: St. Martins, 1978. Pp.94-99, 242-57.

Taylor, Maxwell. <u>The Uncertain Trumpet</u>. Westport, CN: Greenwood, 1974. Pp. 23-79.

Thaxter, Richard. "Nuclear War by Computer Chip: How America Almost Launched on Warning." <u>Progressive</u>, August 1980, pp. 29-30.

Thurow, Lester. "Absorbing a Defense Buildup?" <u>Business Week</u>, June 8, 1981, pp. 110-11.

Thurow, Lester. "The Arms Race and the Economic Order." In: <u>Catholics and Nuclear War</u>. Edited by Philip J. Murnion. New York: Crossroad Publishing, 1983. pp 204-13.

Tirman, John. "The Defense-Economy Debate," pp. 1-32. In: <u>The Militarization of High Technology</u>. Cambridge, MA: Ballinger, 1986.

United Nations. <u>Reduction of Military Budget--International Reporting of Military Expenditures</u>. New York: United Nations, 1983.

U.S. Congress. Congressional Budget Office. "The Survivability of U.S. Forces." In: <u>Counterforce Issues for the U.S. Strategic Forces</u>, pp. 9-21. Washington, DC: Government Printing Office, 1978.

U.S. Executive Office of the President. <u>Report of the President's Commission on Strategic Forces</u>. Washington, DC: Government Printing Office, 1983. pp. 10-22. (2)

Wallace, Michael. "Armaments and Escalation." <u>International Studies Quarterly</u> 26 (1982): 37-56.

Wilson, Pete. "The President's Foundering Strategic Modernization Plan." Strategic Review 13 (Summer 1985): 9-13.

Woodmansee, John et al. The World of a Giant Corporation: Report from the G.E. Project. Seattle: North Country Press, 1975.

Yergin, Daniel. "The Arms Zealots." Harpers, June 1977, pp. 64-76.

EFFECTS OF NUCLEAR WEAPONS:

This section includes discussion of physical, biological, atmospheric, psychological, environmental and other health effects of exploding or stockpiling nuclear weapons, with reference to nuclear winter. Also included are explanations of basic principles of nuclear physics and engineering concerning generation of heat, explosions, radiation and blast effects of fission, fusion and combined reactions.

Abrams, Herbert L., and William Von Kaenel. "Medical Problems of Survivors of Nuclear War: Infection and the Spread of Communicable Diseases." New England Journal of Medicine (November 12, 1981): 1226-32. (2)

American Psychiatric Association. Psychosocial Aspects of Nuclear Developments. Task Force Report No. 20. Washington, DC: American Psychiatric Association, 1982.

Ball, Desmond. "The Control of Damage in Nuclear War." In: Can Nuclear War be Controlled? Adelphi Paper 169. London: International Institute for Strategic Studies, 1981.

Beardslee, William, and John Mack. "The Impact on Children and Adolescents of Nuclear Developments." Psychosocial Aspects of Nuclear Developments. Task Force Report No. 20. Washington, DC: American Psychiatric Association, 1982. pp. 64-93.

Carey, Michael. "Psychological Fallout." Bulletin of Atomic Scientists 38 (January 1982): 20-24.

Carnesale, Albert. "Reviving the ABM Debate." Arms Control Today 11 (April 1981): 1-4.

Bibliography

Carrier, May Gore, et al. "Symposium on Nuclear Winter." _Issues in Science and Technology_ 1 (Winter 1985): 114-33.

Carson, Mark J. "Global Consequences of Nuclear Weaponry." _Annual Review of Nuclear Science_ 26 (1976): 51-87.

Cassel, Christine, et al. _Nuclear Weapons and Nuclear War: A Sourcebook for Health Professionals_. Westport, CT: Praeger, 1984.

Committee for the Compilation of Materials on Damage Caused by the Atomic Bombs in Hiroshima and Nagasaki. _Hiroshima and Nagasaki: The Physical, Medical, and Social Effects of the Atomic Bombings_. Translated by Eisei Ishikawa and David L. Swain. New York: Basic Books, 1981.

Daugherty, William, Barbara Levi and Frank Von Hippel. "The Consequences of 'Limited' Nuclear Attacks on the United States." _International Security_ 10 (Spring 1986): 3-45.

"Effects of Nuclear War." _Journal of the Federation of American Scientists Public Interest Report_ 34 (1963).

Ehrlich, Paul, et al. _The Cold and the Dark: The World After Nuclear War_. New York: Norton, 1985.

Ehrlich, Paul R., et al. "Long Term Biological Consequences of Nuclear War." _Science_ 222 (1983): 1293-1300.

Frank, Jerome D. "Nuclear Arms and Prenuclear Leaders: Sociopsychological Aspects of the Nuclear Arms Race." _Political Psychology_ 4 (1983): 393-408.

Frank, Jerome D. _Sanity and Survival: Psychological Aspects of War and Peace_. New York: Vintage Books, 1968. (2)

Fried, J.H.E. "Law and Nuclear War." _Bulletin of Atomic Scientists_ 38 (June-July 1982): 67-68.

Gardiner, Robert. _The Cool Arm of Destruction: Modern Weapons and Moral Insensitivity_. Philadelphia: Westminster Press, 1972.

Glasstone, S., and A. Dolan. Effects of Nuclear Weapons, 3d. Washington, DC: Government Printing Office, 1977. (5)

Gray, Colin S. "The Nuclear Winter Thesis and U.S. Strategic Policy." Washington Quarterly 8 (Summer 1985): 85-96.

Grinspoon, Lester. The Long Darkness: Psychological and Moral Perspectives on Nuclear Issues. New Haven: Yale University Press, 1986.

Group for the Advancement of Psychiatry. Psychiatric Aspects of the Prevention of Nuclear War. New York: Group for the Advancement of Psychiatry, 1963. pp. 245-56.

Hall, Francoise. "The United States Search for Security: A Psychotherapist's Viewpoint." Journal of Peace Research 20 (1983): 299-311.

Harvard Educational Review. "Education and the Threat of Nuclear War." 54 (1984): Special Issue.

Inglis, David R. Nuclear Energy: Its Physics and Its Social Challenge. Reading MA: Addison-Wesley, 1973.

Jaspers, K. The Future of Mankind. Chicago: University of Chicago Press, 1961. Pp. vii-xi, 1-56.

Katz, Arthur. Economic and Social Consequences of Nuclear Attacks on the United States. Joint Committee on Defense Production, Congress of the United States. Washington, DC: Government Printing Office, 1979, pp. 1-27.

Katz, Arthur. Life After Nuclear War: The Economic and Social Impacts of Nuclear Attacks on the United States. Cambridge, MA: Ballinger, 1982. (2)

Kull, Steven. "Nuclear Nonsense." Foreign Policy 58 (Spring 1985): 28-53. (2)

Lewis, Kevin. "The Prompt and Delayed Effects of Nuclear War." Scientific American. 241 (July 1979): 35-47. (5)

Lifton, Robert J. "Beyond Psychic Numbing." Mobius 4 (January 1984): 46-55. (2)

Bibliography

Lifton, Robert J. "The First Step: Awareness." **New Boston Review**, November/December, 1981.

Lifton, Robert Jay. "In a Dark Time..." In: **The Last Epidemic: Physicians and Scientists on Nuclear War**, pp. 7-20. Chicago: University of Chicago Press, 1981.

Lifton, Robert Jay, and Kai Erikson. "Nuclear War's Effect on the Mind." **New York Times**, March 15, 1982.

McNaught, L. W. **Nuclear Weapons and Their Effects**. Washington, DC: Brassey's Defense Publishers, 1984.

Mack, John E. "Psychological Effects of the Nuclear Arms Race." **Bulletin of Atomic Scientists** 37 (April 1981): 18-23.
Macy, Joanna. **Despair and Personal Power in the Nuclear Age**. Philadelphia: New Society Publishers, 1983.

Mandelbaum, Michael. "The Bomb, Dread, and Eternity." **International Security** 5 (Fall 1980): 3-23.

Metzger, Roger. "Cruise Missiles." In: **Negotiating Security: An Arms Control Reader**. Edited by William Kincade and Jeffrey D. Porro. Washington, DC: Carnegie, 1979.

National Academy of Sciences, National Academy of Engineering, National Research Council. **Proceedings of a Symposium on Postattack Recovery from Nuclear War**. Washington, DC: Government Printing Office, 1968, pp. 3-21, 107-137, 395-497.

Peterson, J. **The Aftermath: The Human and Ecological Consequences of Nuclear War**. New York: Random House, 1983.

Rosenblatt, Roger. "Looking Straight at the Bomb." **Time**, July 6, 1981, pp. 79-80.

Sagan, Carl. "Nuclear War and Climatic Catastrophe: Some Policy Implications." **Foreign Affairs** 62 (Winter 1983/84): 257-292. (3)

Sagan, Scott. "Nuclear Alerts and Crisis Management." **International Security** 9 (1985): 99-139. (2)

Sartori, Leo. "Effects of Nuclear Weapons." **Physics Today**, March 1983, pp. 32-38. (2)

Schneidman, Edwin S. *Deaths of Man*. Baltimore: Penguin Books, 1974. pp. 179-98.

Selden, Robert W. *An Introduction to Fission Explosives*. Livermore, CA: Lawrence Radiation Laborotory, 1969.

Silberner, Joanne. "Psychological A-Bomb Wounds." *Science News*, November 7, 1981, pp. 296-98.

Thompson, James A. *Psychological Aspects of Nuclear War*. New York: Wiley, 1985.

Turco, R.P., et al. "Nuclear Winter: Global Consequences of Multiple Nuclear Explosions." *Science* 222 (1983): 1283-92. (2)

U.S. Department of Defense. "The Potential Effects of Nuclear War on the Climate: A Report to the United States Congress, March 1985." *Survival* 27 (May/June 1985): 130-134.

U.S. Office of Technology Assessment. *The Effects of Nuclear War*. Washington, DC: Government Printing Office, 1979. (2)

Upton, Arthur C. "The Biological Effects of Low-Level Ionizing Radiation." *Scientific American*, February 1982, pp. 41-49.

Vandercook, William F. "Making the Very Best of the Very Worst." *International Security* 11 (Summer 1986): 184-95.

Verdon-Roe, Vivienne. "Growing Up in the Nuclear Age: What Children Can Tell Us." *East-West Journal* (January 1983).

White, Ralph K. *Psychology and the Prevention of Nuclear War*. New York: New York University Press, 1986.

Woodward, Patricia. "How do the American People Feel About the Atomic Bomb?" *Journal of Social Issues* (Winter 1948).

Wohlstetter. A. "Bishops, Statesmen, and Other Strategists on the Bombing of Innocents." *Commentary* (June 1983): 15-35.

Bibliography

Worchel, Stephen, and Joel Cooper. <u>Understanding Social Psychology</u>. Chicago, IL: Dorsey, 1987.

FORCE COMPARISONS:

This section includes discussion of methods and reasons for measuring and comparing nuclear and non-nuclear forces of adversaries, with reference to sources and reliability of available information.

Aspin, Les. "Debate Over US Strategic Forecasts: A Mixed Record." <u>Strategic Review</u> 8 (Summer 1980): 29-42.

Baugh, William. <u>The Politics of Nuclear Balance: Ambiguity and Continuity in Strategic Policies</u>. White Plains, NY: Longman, 1983.

Betts, Richard. "Elusive Equivalence." In: <u>The Strategic Imperative: New Policies for American Security</u>, pp. 108-19. Edited by Samuel P. Huntington. Cambridge, MA: Ballinger, 1982.

Brewer, Garry D., and Bruce Blair. "War Games and National Security with a Grain of SALT." <u>Bulletin of Atomic Scientists</u> 35 (June 1979): 18-26.

Brown, Thomas. "Number Mysticism, Rationality and the Strategic Balance." <u>Orbis</u> 21 (Fall 1977): 479-96.

Brown, Thomas. "US and Soviet Strategic Force Levels, Problems of Assessment and Measurement." <u>Annals of the American Academy of Political and Social Science</u> 457 (September 1981): 18-27.

Center for Defense Information. "U.S. Military Facts." <u>Defense Monitor</u> 11 (1982).

Cordesman, Anthony. "Measuring the Strategic Balance." <u>Comparative Strategy</u> 3 (1982): 187-218.

Evangelista, Matthew. "Stalin's Postwar Army Reappraised." <u>International Security</u> 7 (Winter 1982-83): 110-38. (2)

International Institute for Strategic Studies. <u>Military Balance, 1980-81</u>. Boulder, CO: Westview, 1980.

Levi, Barbara. "Nuclear Arsenals of the US and USSR." Physics Today, March 1983, pp. 43-49. (2)

Nacht, Michael. The Age of Vulnerability. Washington, DC: Brookings, 1985.

Stockholm International Peace Research Institute (SIPRI). World Armaments and Disarmament: SIPRI Yearbook. Philadelphia: Taylor & Francis, 1985.

Thompson, W. Scott. "The Persian Gulf and the Correlation of Forces." International Security 7 (1982): 157-80. (2)

U.S. Department of Defense. Annual Report for Fiscal Year 1986. Washington, DC: Government Printing Office, 1985 (annual). (3)

U.S. Department of Defense, Joint Chiefs of Staff. United States Military Posture for FY 1986. Washington, DC: Government Printing Office, 1985 (annual).

NUCLEAR WEAPONS TECHNOLOGY:

This section includes discussion of technologies and capabilities of various nuclear weapons and delivery systems. Basic discussions of physical principles of nuclear physics and engineering will be found with materials on the environmental and health Effects of Nuclear Weapons, above.

Anson, Robert Sam. "The Neutron Bomb." New York Times, August 5, 1977, pp. 24-32.

Arkin, William M., Thomas B. Cockran and Milton M. Hoenig. "Resource Paper on the US Nuclear Arsenal." Bulletin of Atomic Scientists (August/September, 1984): 3s-15s.

Barker, Robert. "Debate on a Comprehensive Nuclear Test Ban, Con." Physics Today, August 1983, pp. 25-34.

Bigelow, Albert S. "Why I am Sailing into the Pacific Bomb Test Area." In: Seeds of Liberation, pp. 144-50. Edited by Paul Goodman. New York: George Braziller, 1964.

Bibliography

Blackett, Patrick M. "The Role of Two Scientists in Government." _Scientific American_, April, 1961.

Blanchard, William H. _Aggression American Style_. Santa Monica, CA: Goodyear Publishing, 1978.

Brim, Raymond E., and Patricia Condon. "Another A-Bomb Coverup." _Washington Monthly_, January, 1981, pp. 45-49.

Bullard, "The Detection of Underground Explosions." _Scientific American_, July, 1966, pp. 19-29.

Center for Defense Information. "MX: The Weapon Nobody Wants." _Defense Monitor_ 10 (1981).

Cockran, Thomas B., William M. Arkin, and Milton M. Hoenig. "Glossary of Terms" and "Nuclear Weapons Primer," pp. 314-27 and pp. 322-35. In: _Nuclear Weapons Databook Vol 1: US Nuclear Forces and Capabilities_. Cambridge, MA: Ballinger, 1984.

Cohen, S.T. "Enhanced Radiation Warheads: Setting the Record Straight." _Strategic Review_ 6 (Winter 1978): 9-17.

Daggett, S. _The New Generation of Nuclear Weapons_. Washington, DC: Institute for Policy Studies, 1980.

Day, Samuel H., Jr. "The Neutron Bomb Lives After All." _Progressive_, October 1978, pp. 28-29.

Dewitt, Hugh E. "Debate on a Comprehensive Nuclear Test Ban." _Physics Today_, August 1983, pp. 25-34.

Ehrlich, Robert. _Waging Nuclear Peace: The Technology and Politics of Nuclear Weapons_. Albany: SUNY Press, 1984.

Ellsberg, Daniel. "There Must Be No Neutron Bomb." _The Nation_, May 27, 1978, pp.632-3.

Feld, Bernard T., and Kosta Tsipis. "Land-Based Intercontinental Ballistic Missiles." _Scientific American_, November 1979, pp. 55-61. (3)

Gray, Colin S. "NATO Strategy and the 'Neutron Bomb'." _Policy Review_ 7 (Winter 1979): 7-26.

"The Heart of the Explosion." The Economist, September 1, 1984, pp. 3-11.

Hodsden, William H. "Atomic Bomb Test Veteran." In: Nuclear Witness: Insiders Speak Out, pp. 171-205. Edited by Leslie J. Freeman. New York: W.W. Norton, 1981.

Holloway, David. "Research Note: Soviet Thermonuclear Development." International Security 4 (1979-80): 192-197.

Kahn, Herman. On Thermonuclear War. Westport CT: Greenwood, 1978.

Kaplan, Fred. "Cruise Missile: Wonder Weapon or Dud?" High Technology, February, 1983. pp. 16-34.

Kincade, William H. "Over the Technological Horizan." Daedalus 10 (Winter 1981): 105-127.

Kincade, William. "Will MX Backfire?" Foreign Policy 37 (1979-80): 43-58.

Kistiakowsky, George B. "Weaponry: The Folly of the Neutron Bomb." Atlantic, June 1978, pp. 4-14.

Korb, Lawrence J. "The Case for the MX." Air Force Review 21 (1980): 3-10.

Morland, Howard. "The H-Bomb Secret." Progressive, September 1979, pp. 14-23.

Myers, Henry R. "Extending the Nuclear Test Ban." Scientific American, January, 1972, 13-23.

"Myth of ICBM Vulnerability." Defense Week, August 11, 1980, pp.4-5.

Scoville, Herbert, Jr. "Missile Submarines and National Security." Scientific American, June, 1972, pp. 15-27.

Scoville, Herbert, Jr. MX: Prescription for Disaster. Cambridge, MA: MIT Press, 1981.

Summer, Theo. "The Neutron Bomb: Nuclear War Without Tears." Survival 14 (1977): 263-266.

Bibliography

Toomay, John.   "Technical Characteristics."   In:
Cruise Missiles: Technology, Strategy, Politics. Edited by Richard K. Betts. Washington, DC: Brookings,
1981.

Tsipis, Kosta.   "The Accuracy of Strategic Missiles."
Scientific American, July 1975. (2)

United Nations, Secretary-General.   Nuclear Weapons.
Brookline, MA: Autumn Press, 1980.

U.S. Congress. Senate.   The Interim Report of the
Nunn-Warner Work ing Group.   98th Cong., 1st sess.,
1983.

US Executive Office of the President.   Report of the
President's Commission on Strategic Forces [Scowcroft
Commission].   Washington DC: Government Printing Of-
fice, 1983.

U.S. Office of Technology Assessment.   MX Missile Bas-
ing.   Washington, DC: Government Printing Office,
1981. (2)

Van Cleave, William.   "Nuclear Technology and Weapons."
In: Nuclear Proliferation: Phase II. Edited by Robert M. Lawrence and Joel Larus.   Lawrence, KS: University Press of Kansas, 1974.

Walker, Paul F.   "New Weapons and the Changing Nature
of Warfare." Arms Control Today 9 (April 1979).

Walker, P.   "Precision-Guided Weapons."   Scientific
Aamerican, August 1981.

Wisner, Kent F.   "Military Aspects of Enhanced Radiation Weapons." Survival 23 (November-December 1981):
246.

Wit, Joel S.   "Advances in Anti-Submarine Warfare."
Scientific American, February 1981, pp. 31-41. (4)

York, Herbert R.   "The Debate over the Hydrogen Bomb."
Scientific American, October 1975, pp. 106-113.

Zseiburg, Seymour L.   "MX: Why Do We Need It?"   Defense 80 (1980): 16 pp.

CONVENTIONAL WEAPONS:

This section includes discussion of non-nuclear weapons systems chemical and biological warfare, techniques of saturation bombing, battlefield emplacements, and mandatory military service (the draft).

Cookson. A Survey of Biological and Chemical Warfare. New York: Monthly Review Press, 1969.

Douhet, Guillo. The Command of the Air. Washington, DC: Government Printing Office, 1983. pp. 3-92.

Epstein, Joshua M. "Soviet Vulnerabilities in Iran and the RDF Deterrent." International Security 6 (1981): 126-58. (2)

Foley, W., and V. Soedel. "Ancient Oared Warships." Scientific American, March 1979, pp. 150-57.

Johnson, Chalmers. Autopsy on People's War. Berkeley: University of California Press, 1974.

Kaufmann, William W. Planning Conventional Forces. Washington DC: Brookings, 1982.

Lacy, James. "The Case for Conscription." In: Military Service In the United States. Edited by Brendt Scowcroft. Englewood Cliffs, NJ: Prentice-Hall, 1982.

Littauer. Air War in Indochina. Boston: Beacon Press, 1971.

McNaugher, Thomas. "Balancing Soviet Power in the Persian Gulf." The Brookings Review 1 (1983): 20-24.

Meselson, M., and J. Perry Robinson. "Chemical Warfare and Chemical Disarmament." Scientific American, April 1980, pp.38-47. (4)

Soedel, V., and W. Foley. "Ancient Catapults." Scientific American, March 1979, pp. 150-57. (3)

U.S. Congress. Congressional Budget Office. Rapid Deployment Forces: Policy and Budgetary Implications. Washington, DC: Government Printing Office, 1983. (2)

Bibliography

DEFENSIVE SYSTEMS:

This section includes discussion of defensive weapons system technologies (e.g. antiballistic missles: ABM, ballistic missle defense: BDM) and management measures (civil defense, evacuation plans) developed in preparation for a potential nuclear war.

For a recent, comprehensive guide to the literature of the debate over President Reagan's Strategic Defense Initiative, see: Robert M. Lawrence, Strategic Defense Initiative: Bibliography and Research Guide. Boulder, CO: Westview Press, 1987.

Aspin, Les. "Soviet Civil Defense: Myth and Reality." In: Willaim Kincaide and Jeffrey D. Porro, Negotiating Security: An Arms Control Reader. Washington, DC: Carnegie, 1979. pp. 104-11.

Balaschak, Mark, Gordan MacDonald, and Jack Ruina. "Soviet Strategic Air Defense." In: Cruise Missiles: Technology, Strategy, Politics. Edited by Richard K. Betts. Washington, DC: Brookings, 1981.

Beres, Louis Rene. "Subways to Armaggeddon." Society (Transaction) 20 (September/October 1983): 7-10.

Bethe, Hans, et al. "Space-Based Ballistic Missile Defense." Scientific American 251 (October 1984): 39-49.

Broad, William. Star Warriors. New York: Simaon & Schuster, 1985.

Brown, Harold. "The Strategic Defense Initative: Defensive Systems and Strategic Debates." Survival 27 (March/April 1985): 55-64. (3)

Brzezinski, Z. Promise or Peril: The Strategic Defense Initiative. Washignton, DC: Ethics and Public Policy Center, 1986.

Carnesale, Albert. "The Strategic Defense Initiative." In: American Defense Annual: 1985-86, pp. 187-205. Edited by George Hudson and Joseph Kruzel. Lexington, MA: Lexington Books, 1986.

Carter, Ashton, and David N. Schwartz, eds. Ballistic Missile Defense. Washington, DC: Brookings, 1984.

Drell, S., P. Farley, and D. Holloway. "Preserving the ABM Treaty: A Critique of the Reagan Strategic Defense Initiative." International Security 8 (Fall 1984): 51-92.

Garwin, Gottfried. "Antisatellite Weapons." Scientific American, June 1984, pp. 45-55.

Garwin, Richard. "ASW and National Security." Scientific American, July 1972, pp. 14-25.

Garwin, Richard, and Hans Bethe. "Anti-Ballistic Missile Systems." Scientific American, March 1968, pp. 21-31.

Geiger, H. Jack. "The Illusion of Survival." Bulletin of Atomic Scientists 37 (June/July 1981): 16-21.

Glaser, C. "Do We Want the Missile Defenses We Can Build?" International Security 9 (Summer 1985): 25-57.

Gray, Colin S. "A Case for Strategic Defense." Survival 27 (1985): 50-55. Also pp. 81-87 in: Strategic Defense Initiative: Folly or Future? Edited by P. Edward Haley and Jack Merritt. Boulder, CO: Westview Press, 1986.

Haley, P. Edward, and Jack Merritt, eds. Strategic Defense Initiative: Folly or Future? Boulder, CO: Westview Press, 1986.

Holton, James L. "In Defense of Civil Defense." Society 20 (1983): 11-13.

Huntley, Henry C. "Postattack Survival." Society 20 (1983): 13-16.

Jastrow, Robert. "Reagan vs the Scientists: Why the President is Right About Missile Defense." Commentary, January 1984, pp. 25-32. (2)

Klass, Philip J. "Laser Destroys Missile in Test." Aviation Week and Space Technology, August 7, 1978.

Klinghoffer, Max. "Suicide or Medical Preparedness?" Society 20 (1983): 18-21.

Bibliography

Koppes, Clayton R. "The Militarization of the American Space Program: An Historical Perspective." _Virginia Quarterly Review_ 60 (Winter 1984): 1-20.

Nitze, Paul. "Civil Defense--The New Debate." _Worldview_ 22 (January-February 1979): 40-41.

Nitze, Paul. "SDI and the ABM Treaty." Current Policy 711 Washington, DC: U.S. Department of State, 1985.

Orberg, James. "Weapons [in orbit]." _Science Digest_, April, 1984, pp. 41-45, 96.

Panofsky, Wolfgang. "The Strategic Defense Initiative: Perception vs Reality." _Physics Today_, June 1985, pp. 34-45. (2)

Parmentola, John, and Kosta Tsipis. "Particle Beam Weapons," _Scientific American_, April 1979, pp. 54-65. (4)

"President Reagan's Civil Defense Program." _Defense Monitor_ 11 (1982): 1-8.

Reagan, Ronald. "Address to the Nation: Peace and National Security." _New York Times_, March 23, 1983. (3)

Robinson, Clarence A. "US Pushes Development of Beam." _Aviation Week and Space Technology_, February 9, 1981.

Robinson, Clarence A. "Layered Defense System Pushed to Protect ICBM's." _Aviation Week and Space Technology_, February 9, 1981.

Teller, Edward. "Dangerous Myths About Nuclear Arms." _Reader's Digest_, November 1982, pp. 139-144.

Thompson, E.P., ed. _Star Wars_. New York: Pantheon, 1985.

Totter, John R. "Our Sisyphean Task." _Society_ 20 (1983): 16-18.

Tsipis, Kosta. "Laser Weapons." _Scientific American_ 245 (December 1981): 51-57. (3)

Union of Concerned Scientists. The Fallacy of Star Wars. Cambridge, MA: Union of Concerned Scientists, 1984.

U.S. Congress. House. Armed Services Committee. Recent False Alerts from the Nation's Missile Attack Warning System. Washington, DC: Government Printing Office, 1980.

U.S. Congress. Office of Technology Assessment. Ballistic Missile Defense Technologies. Washington, DC: Government Printing Office, 1985. (2)

U.S. Department of Defense. Report to the Congress on the Strategic Defense Initiative, 1985. Washington, DC: Government Printing Office, 1984.

Van Cleave, William R. Fortress USSR: The Soviet Strategic Defense Initiative and the US Strategic Defense Response. Palo Alto: Hoover Institution Press, 1986.

Von Hippel, Frank. "The Myths of Edward Teller." Bulletin of Atomic Scientists 39 (March 1983): 6-12.

Weinstein, John. "Soviet Civil Defense: The Mine Shaft Gap Revisited." Arms Control Today 12 (July/August 1982).

Wiebers, David O. "The Ultimate Appeasement." Society 20 (1983): 24-26.

Winter, Metta. "Survivalism in the Schools." Nuclear Times, March 1983, pp. 16-17.

Yonas, Gerold. "Strategic Defense Initiative: The Politics and Science of Space Weapons." Physics Today, June,1985, pp. 24-32. (2)

COMMAND, CONTROL COMMUNICATIONS AND INTELLIGENCE:

This section includes discussion of the role of command, control, communications and intelligence (C3I) systems in deterring and fighting a nuclear war, with consideration of technologies available and effects of nuclear detonations on those systems.

Blair, Bruce. Strategic Command and Control. Washington, DC: Brookings, 1985.

Bibliography

Bloomfield, Lincoln. "Nuclear Crisis and Human Frailty." _Bulletin of Atomic Scientists_ 40 (October 1985): 26-30.

Carter, Ashton B. "The Command and Control of Nuclear War." _Scientific American_, January, 1985, pp. 32-39. (2)

Godson, Roy, ed. _Intelligence Requirements for the 1980's_. Lexington, MA: Lexington Books, 1985.

Morse and Kimball. "How to Hunt a Submarine." In: _The World of Mathematics_, vol.4, pp. 2160-79. Edited by James R. Newman. New York: Simon & Schuster, 1956.

Steinbrunner, John. "Nuclear Decapitation." _Foreign Policy_ 46 (1981-82): 16-28. (2)

Van Creveld, Martin. _Command in War_. Cambridge, MA: Harvard University Press, 1985. pp. 1-17, 148-275.

Van Creveld, Martin. _Supplying War: Logistics from Wallenstein to Patton_. Cambridge, MA: Harvard University Press, 1979. pp. 1-3; 142-237.

NUCLEAR ETHICS:

This section includes discussion of moral, ethical and religious dimensions of stockpiling nuclear arms, with statements by various organized religions on nuclear weapons and war.

Alexander, Leo. "Medical Science Under Dictatorship." _New England Journal of Medicine_ 241 (14 July 1949): 39-47.

Beitz, Charles R., ed. _International Ethics_. Princeton: Princeton University Press, 1985.

Bettelheim, Bruno. _Surviving and Other Essays_. New York: Vintage, 1980. pp. 3-18, 246-57.

Brandt, R.B. "Utilitarianism and the Rules of War." _Philosophy and Public Affairs_. 1 (Winter 1972).

Buhle, Paul, and Thomas Fieher. "Socialism and Spirituality." _Monthly Review_ 37 (November 1985): 9-20.

Cohen, M. _War and Moral Responsibility_. Princeton, NJ: Princeton University Press, 1973.

Eardlin, Russell. "Unilateral Versus Mutual Disarmament." _Philosophy and Public Affairs_ 12 (Summer 1983).

Ford, J.C., and S.J. Ford. "The Morality of Obliteration Bombing." In: _War and Morality_. Edited by Richard Wasserstrom. Belmont, CA: Wadsworth Press, 1970.

French and German Bishops. _Out of Justice, Peace and Winning the Peace_. Ignatius Press, n.d.

Friedman, Thomas L. "No Illusions: Israel Reassesses Its Chances for Peace." _New York Times Magazine_, 26 January 1986.

Gabriel, Richard. _To Serve With Honor: A Treatise on Military Ethics and the Way of the Soldier_. Westport, CT: Greenwood Press, 1982.

Gallie, W.B. _Philosophers of War and Peace_. New York: Cambridge University Press, 1979.

Galtung, J. _The True Worlds, A Transnational Perspective._ Boulder, CO: Westview Press, 1981.

Hampshire, S. _Morality and Pessimism_. New York: Cambridge University Press, 1972.

Hardin, Russell, et al, eds. _Nuclear Deterrence: Ethics and Strategy_. Chicago: University of Chicago Press, 1985.

Heilbroner, Robert L. _An Inquiry into the Human Prospect_. New York: Norton, 1980.

Hilberg, Raul. "The Nature of the Process." In: _Survivors, Victims and Perpetrators_, pp. 5-46. Edited by J. Dimsdale. New York: Hemisphere Publishing, 1980.

Hirsh, A. "A Jewish View of Nuclear Weapons." _Theology Today_ 34 (1980): 24-29.

Hollins, H. B. "A Defensive Weapons System." _Bulletin of Atomic Scientists_ 38 (June-July 1982): 63-65.

Bibliography

Kavka, Gregory. _Moral Paradoxes of Nuclear Deterrence_.
New York: Cambridge University Press, 1987.

Kristamurti, I.J. _Talks and Dialogues_. New York:
Avon, 1976.

Lackey, Douglas. "Missiles and Morals: A Utilitarian
Looks at Nuclear Deterrence." _Philosophy and Public
Affairs_ 11 (Summer 1982).

Lackey, Douglas. "Disarmament Revisited: A Reply to
Ravaka and Hardin." _Philosophy and Public Affairs_ 12
(Summer 1983): 261-265.

Lifton, Robert Jay. "The Concept of the Survivor."
In: _Survivors, Victims and Perpetrators_, pp. 113-24.
Edited by J. Dimsdale. New York: Hemisphere Publish-
ing, 1980.

More, Sir Thomas. _Utopia_. In: _The Complete Works of
Sir Thomas More_. New Haven: Yale University Press,
1965.

Murnian. Philip, ed. _Catholics and Nuclear War: A
Commentary on the U.S. Catholic Bishops Pastoral Letter
on War and Peace_. New York: Crossroad, 1983. (2)

Nagel, Thomas. "War and Massacre." In: _War and Moral Responsibility_. Edited by Marshall Cohen, et al.
Princeton, NJ: Princeton University Press, 1974.(2)

Novak, Michael. _Moral Clarity in the Nuclear Age_.
Nashville: Thomas Nelson, 1983.

Nye, Joseph S., Jr. _Nuclear Ethics_. New York: Free
Press, 1986. (2)

O'Brian, William. _Theological Studies_ 44 (1983):
191-220.

Peters, Rudolph. _Jihad in Medieaval and Modern Islam_.
Leiden: E.J. Brill, 1977. pp. 1-90.

Rubenstein, Richard L. "The Political Significance of
Latin American Liberation Theology." _World Affairs_ 148
(Winter 1985/86): 159-67.

Shulstad, Raymond A. <u>Peace is My Profession: A Sol-dier's View of the Moral Dimension of US Nuclear Poli-cy</u>. Washington, DC: National Defense University, 1986.

Sterba, James P., ed. <u>The Ethics of War and Nuclear Deterrence</u>. Belmont, CA: Wadsworth, 1984. (2)

Tagg, John. "Breakfast With the Bishops: An Anniver-sary." <u>National Review</u>, June 15, 1984, pp. 26, 28-30, 32-34.

Thompson, E.P. "A Letter to America." <u>The Nation</u> 232 (1981): 68-93. (2)

U.S. Catholic Bishops. "The Challenge of Peace: God's Promise and Our Response." <u>Origins</u>, May 19, 1983. (7)

Wakin, Malham, ed. <u>War, Morality and the Military Pro-fession</u>. Boulder, CO: Westview, 1979. (3)

Walzer, Michael. "World War II: Why Was This War Dif-ferent?" In: <u>War and Moral Responsibility.</u> Edited by Marshall Cohen, et al. Princeton, NJ: Princeton Uni-versity Press, 1974.

Wernik, Jankiel. "A Year in Treblinka." In: <u>The Death Camp Treblinka</u>, pp. 147-88. Edited by Alexander Donat. New York: Holocost Library, 1979.

Wilson, Andrew. <u>The Disarmers Handbook</u>. New York: Penguin Books, 1983.

Yoder, John Howard. "Living the Disarmed Life." <u>So-journers</u>, January, 1985.

ART, MUSIC AND LITERATURE:

This section includes examples of art, music and literature inspired by concerns for war and nuclear weapons, and writings about such materials. Many of the familiar classical works are available from more than one publisher, singly or in collections. A list of films will be found in the section labeled Films be-low.

Bakhtin, M.M. <u>The Dialogic Imagination</u>. Austin: Uni-versity of Texas Press, 1981.

Bibliography

Brians, Paul. <u>Nuclear Holocaust: Atomic War in Fiction, 1945-1982</u>.   Kent, OH: Kent State University Press, 1987,

Brians, Paul.   "Teaching About Nuclear War Through Fiction."   In: <u>Nuclear War Education: A Survey of Different Perspectives and Resources</u>, edited by Robert Ehrlich.   Westport, CN: Greenwood Press, 1987.

Burdick, Eugene, and Harvey Wheeler.   <u>Fail-Safe</u>.   New York: McGraw-Hill, 1962.

Byron, Lord.   <u>Don Juan</u>.   Edited by T.G. Steffan, E. Steffan, and W.W. Pratt.   New Haven: Yale University Press, 1982.

Clough, Arthur Hugh.   <u>Amours de Voyage</u>.   Edited by Patrick Scott.   St. Lucia, Queensland: University of Queensland Press, 1974.

Coover, Robert. "Groun'-Hog Hunt."   <u>American Review</u> 25 (1976): 1-32.

Crane, Stephen.   <u>The Red Badge of Courage</u>.   New York: Bantam Books, 1986.

Erasmus.   <u>The Complaint of Peace</u>.   Chicago: Open Court Publishing, 1974.

Fussell, Paul.   <u>The Great War and Modern Memory</u>.   New York: Oxford University Press, 1977.

Gardner, John.   <u>Grendel</u>.   New York: Ballantine Books, 1978.

Golding, William.   <u>The Lord of the Flies</u>.   New York: Penguin, 1960.

Hoban, Russell.   <u>Riddley Walker</u>.   New York: Washington Square Printers, 1982. (2)

Homer.   <u>Iliad</u>.   Translated by R. Lattimore.   Chicago: University of Chicago Press, 1951.   pp. 418-21.

Kirst, Hans Helmut.   <u>The Seventh Day</u>.   Garden City, NY: Doubleday, 1959.

Kornbluth, C.M.   <u>Not This August</u>.   Garden City, NY: Doubleday, 1955.

Lakoff, George, and Mark Johnson. <u>Metaphors We Live By</u>. Chicago: University of Chicago Press, 1980.

Landor, Walter Savage. <u>Pericles and Aspasia</u>. Boston: Roberts Brothers, 1871.

Maland, Charles. "Dr. Strangelove (1964): Nightmare Comedy and the Ideology of the Liberal Consensus." <u>American Quarterly</u>.

Masuji, Ibusi. <u>Black Rain</u>. Tokyo: Kandansha, International, 1981.

McIntyre, Vonda. <u>Dreamsnake</u>. Boston: Houghton Mifflin, 1978.

McMahon, Thomas. <u>Principles of American Nuclear Chemistry: A Novel</u>. New York: Avon Books, 1970.

Melville, Herman. <u>Billy Budd and Other Tales</u>. New York: Penguin, 1986.

Miller, Walter M., Jr. <u>A Canticle for Leibowitz</u>. Boston: G.K. Hall, 1976. (4)

More, Sir Thomas. <u>Utopia</u>. In: <u>The Complete Works of Sir Thomas More</u>. New Haven, CT: Yale University Press, 1965.

Morris, Edita. <u>The Flowers of Hiroshima</u>. New York: Viking Press, 1959.

O'Brien, Tim. "Civil Defense." <u>Esquire</u>, August 1980, pp. 82, 84-88.

Peacock, Thomas Love. <u>The Misfortunes of Elphin</u>. New York: AMS Press, 1967.

Rabelais, Francois. <u>The Histories of Gargantua and Pantagruel</u>. Book I. Hammondworth, Middlesex: Penguin Books, 1955. chap. 25-58.

Robinson, Kim Stanley. <u>The Wild Shore</u>. New York: Berkeley Publishing Group, 1984.

Sanders, Scott R. "At Play in the Paradise of Bombs." <u>North American Review</u> (September 1983): 53-58.

Bibliography

Seuss, Dr. _The Butter Battle Book_. New York: Random House, 1984.

Shute, Nevil. _On the Beach_. New York: Ballantine, 1977.

Smiley, Jane. "The Blinding Light of the Mind." _Atlantic Monthly_, December 1983, pp. 48, 50-52, 55-58.

Sontag, Susan. "The Imagination of Disaster." In: _Against Interpretation and Other Essays_. New York: Delta Books, 1966.

Taylor, Clarke. "How Hollywood Learned to Stop Worrying and Hate the Bomb." _American Film_, October, 1982.

Titus, A. Constandina. "Back to Ground Zero: Old Footage through New Lenses." _Journal of Popular Film and Television_ 11 (Spring 1983): 3-11.

Tolstoy, Leo. _War and Peace._ New York: Penguin, 1982.

Voloshinov, V.N. _Marxism and the Philosophy of Language_. Cambridge, MA: Harvard University Press, 1986.

Vonnegut, Kurt. _Slaughter-House Five_. New York: Delacourt Press, 1975.

Welsh, James M. "The Modern Apocolypse: The War Game." _Journal of Popular Film and Television_ 11 (Spring 1983): 25-41.

Wilhelm, Kate. _Where Late the Sweet Birds Sang_. New York: Harper & Row, 1976.

Wright, David Henry, tr. _Beowulf_. New York: Penguin, 1976.

FILM

These films were used in courses examined. A more comprehensive list of arms race and nuclear war films may be found in: Karen Sayer and John Dowling, eds. _1984 National Directory of AAV Resources on Nuclear War and the Arms Race_. University of Michigan Media Resources Center, 400 Fourth St., Ann Arbor, MI 48103. $4.

Nuclear Weapons in the University Classroom

Items designated "EFVL" are available from several educational institutions as listed under the item title in: Educational Film/Video Locator of the Consortium of University Film Centers, 3d. New York: R.R. Bowker, 1986.

"A is for Atom, B is for Bomb." (1980). EFVL.

"Atomic Cafe." (1982). Thorn-EMI/HBO Video, 1370 Avenue of the Americas, New York, NY. 212-977-8990. (4)

"Battle of Algiers." International Historic Films, P.O. Box 29035, Chicago, IL. 312-436-8053.

"The Bikinians." (1974). University of Iowa AV Center, Media Library, C-5 East Hall, Iowa City, IA 52242.

"The Building of the Bomb." University of Washington, Educational Media Scheduling Office, 35 D. Kane Hall, DG-10, University of Washington, Seattle, WA. 206-543-9909.

Chrzanowski, Paul L. "Ballistic Missile Defense and Crisis Stability." Livermore, CA: Lawrence Livermore National Laboratory, 1988. 43 Lecture slides.

"Controlling Interest." University of Illinois Film Center, 1325 Oak St., Champaign, IL 61820. 800-367-3456. (2)

"The Day After." Embassy Home Entertainment, 1901 Avenue of the Stars, Los Angeles, CA 90067. 213-553-3600. (3)

"The Day After Trinity: J. Robert Oppenheimer and the Atomic Bomb." (1981). Pyramid Film and Video, Box 1048, Santa Monica, CA 90406. 800-421-2304. (10)

"The Decision to Drop the Bomb." University of Illinois Film Center, 1325 Oak St., Champaign, IL 61820. 800-367-3456. (2)

"Dr. Strangelove, Or How I Learned to Stop Worrying and to Love the Bomb." (1964). RCA/Columbia Pictures Home Video, 2901 W. Alameda Ave., Burbank, CA 91505. 818-954-4590. (6)

Bibliography

"El Salvador-Another Vietnam?" Icarus Films, 200 Park Avenue South, Suite 1319, New York, NY 10003.

"Energy, The Nuclear Alternative." University of Illinois Film Center, 1325 Oak St., Champaign, Il 61820. 800-367-3456.

"Fail Safe." RCA/Columbia Pictures Home Video, 2901 W. Alameda Ave., Burbank, CA 91505. 818-954-4590.

"The False Frontier." (1986). Union of Concerned Scientists, 26 Church St., Cambridge, MA 02258.

"Generations of Resistance." (1980, 1984). EFVL.

"George Kennan: A Critical Voice." Blackwood Productions, 251 West 57th St., New York, NY 10019. 212-247-4710

"Gods of Metal." Icarus Films, 200 Park Ave. South, Siute 1319, New York, NY 10003.

"Hearts and Minds." Embassy Home Entertainment, 1901 Avenue of the Stars, Los Angeles, CA 90067. 213-553-3600.

"Hiroshima-Nagasaki, August 1945." University of Arizona Film Scheduling, Bureau of Audio-Visual Services, University of Arizona, Tucson, AZ. 626-884-3872. (5)

"Hiroshima and Nagasaki: Harvest of Nuclear War." (1982). EFVL.

"How Much is Enough: Decisionmaking in the Nuclear Age." (1982). University of California, Extension Media Center, 2223 Fulton St., Berkeley, CA 94720. 415-642-0460. (2)

"If You Love This Planet." (1982). EFVL.

"Into the Mouths of Babes." CC Films, National Council of Churches, 475 Riverside Dr., Room 860, New York, NY 10115-0050. 212-870-2575.

"Kennedy vs. Kruschev: Missile Showdown." (1965) University of Michigan, The University of Michigan Media Resources Center, 400 Fourth St., Ann Arbor, MI 48103-4816. 313-764-5360. (2)

"The Last Epidemic: Medical Consequences of Nuclear Weapons and Nuclear War." University of Michigan Media Resources Center, 400 Fourth St., Ann Arbor, MI 48103-4816. 313-764-5360. (4)

"The Lost Generation." (1983). EFVL.

"Martin Luther King Jr." University of Colorado. Academic Media Services, Stadium Building, Boulder CO 80309. 303-492-7341.

"Nick Mazzuco: Biography of an Atomic Vet." (1982). Green Mountain Post Films, P.O. Box 229, Turners Falls, MA 01376. (413) 863-4754 or 8248.

"No First Use: Preventing Nuclear War." University of Colorado. Academic Media Services, Stadium Building, Boulder, CO 80309. 303-492-7341.

"No Place to Hide." Prism. 1875 Century Park East, Los Angeles, CA 90067. 213-277-3270.

"Nuclear Countdown." (1978). EFVL.

"Nuclear Nightmares." WNET/Thirteen Non-Broadcast. 3200 Eisenhower Parkway, Ann Arbor, MI 48104. 313-971-3647.

"Nuclear Power Pro and Con." CRM McGraw Hill Films, 674 Via de la Valle, P.O. Box 641, Del Mar, CA 92014. 619-453-5000

"Nuclear Strategy for Beginners." (1983). NOVA. University of Michigan Media Resources Center, 400 Fourth St., Ann Arbor, MI 48103.(2)

"Nuclear War: Guide to Armageddon." Films Inc. Film and Tape Division, 5547 North Ravenswood Ave., Chicago, IL 60640-1199. 800-323-4222. Ext. 43.

"Obedience." University of Washington, Educational Media Collection Scheduling Office. 35 D Kane Hall DG 10, University of Washington, Seattle, WA 98195. 206-543-9909.

"The Portable Phonograph." (1977). EFVL.

Bibliography

"The Real War in Space." Films Inc., Film and Tape Division, 5547 North Ravenswood Ave., Chicago, IL 60640. 800-323-4222. Ext. 43. (2)

"The Red Army." PBS Video, 1320 Braddock Pl. Alexandria, VA 22314-1698. 703-739-5380.

"The Russians." Learning Corporation of America, 108 Wilmot Rd. Deerfield, IL 60015-9990. 312-940-1260.

"Special Bulletin." Karl/Lorimer Home Video, 17942 Cowan Ave., Irvine, CA 92714. 714-474-0355.

"Star Wars: A Search for Security." (2)

"Testament." Paramount Home Video, 5555 Melrose Ave., Los Angeles, CA 90038. 213-468-5000

"Threads" (3)

"Truman and the A-Bomb." Learning Corporation of America, 108 Wilmot Rd. Deerfield, IL 60015-9990. 312-940-1260.

Unforgettable Fire: Pictures Drawn by Atomic Bomb Survivors. Japanese Broadcasting Company.

"US vs. USSR: Who's Ahead?" University of Michigan Media Resources Center, 400 Fourth St., Ann Arbor, MI 48103-4816. 313-764-5360.

"Visions of Star Wars." Nova/Frontline

"The War Game." International Historic Films, P.O. Box 29035, Chicago, IL. 312-436-8051.(6)

"War Without Winners." Verve Films Inc. 733 Green Bay Rd. Wilmette, IL 60091. 800-323-1406. (3)

"Who's in Charge Here?" New York State Education Department, Center for Learning Technologies, Media Distribution Network, Room C-7, Concourse Level, Cultural Education Center, Albany, NY 12230. 518-474-3168.

"Z" (1969). University of Texas-Dallas, Health Science Center, 5323 Harry Hines Blvd., Dallas, TX 75235.

ABOUT THE CONTRIBUTORS

Michael S. Hamilton, Ph.D. Colorado State University, is Assistant Professor of Political Science at the University of Southern Maine. He teaches International Relations, Public Policy Making, Public Administration, Environmental Politics, and has research interests concerning all portions of the nuclear fuel cycle.

William A. Lindeke, Ph.D. Claremont Graduate School, is Associate Professor of Political Science at the University of Lowell, Massachusetts. He teaches political science courses in Defense and Disarmament, Comparative Politics, and has research interests concerning military mobilization and demobilization in developing countries.

John MacDougall, Ph.D. Harvard University, is Professor of Sociology and Coordinator of Peace and Conflict Studies at the University of Lowell, Massachusetts. He teaches an interdisciplinary course on Nuclear Weapons, Values and Society, and has lived in the Soviet Union and India. He has written on arms control movements in the United States and ethnic movements in India.

1406